THE PRINCETON REVIEW

WRITING SMART

YOUR GUIDE TO GREAT WRITING

D1024281

BOOKS IN THE PRINCETON REVIEW SERIES

Cracking the ACT
Cracking the ACT with Sample Tests on CD-ROM
Cracking the CLEP (College-Level Examination
  Program)
Cracking the GED
Cracking the GMAT
Cracking the GMAT with Sample Tests
  on Computer Disk
Cracking the GRE
Cracking the GRE with Sample Tests
  on Computer Disk
Cracking the GRE Biology Subject Test
Cracking the GRE Literature in English
  Subject Test
Cracking the GRE Psychology Subject Test
Cracking the LSAT
Cracking the LSAT with Sample Tests
  on Computer Disk
Cracking the LSAT with Sample Tests on CD-ROM
Cracking the MAT (Miller Analogies Test)
Cracking the SAT and PSAT
Cracking the SAT and PSAT with Sample Tests
  on Computer Disk
Cracking the SAT and PSAT with Sample Tests
  on CD-ROM
Cracking the SAT II: Biology Subject Test
Cracking the SAT II: Chemistry Subject Test
Cracking the SAT II: English Subject Tests
Cracking the SAT II: French Subject Test
Cracking the SAT II: History Subject Tests
Cracking the SAT II: Math Subject Tests
Cracking the SAT II: Physics Subject Test
Cracking the SAT II: Spanish Subject Test
Cracking the NTE
Cracking the TOEFL with Audiocassette
Flowers & Silver MCAT
Flowers Annotated MCAT
Flowers Annotated MCATs with Sample Tests
  on Computer Disk
Flowers Annotated MCATs with Sample Tests
  on CD-ROM

Culturescope Grade School Edition
Culturescope High School Edition
Culturescope College Edition

LSAT/GRE Analytic Workout
SAT Math Workout
SAT Verbal Workout

All U Can Eat
Don't Be a Chump!
How to Survive Without Your Parents' Money
Speak Now!
Trashproof Resumes

Biology Smart
Grammar Smart
Math Smart
Reading Smart
Study Smart
Word Smart: Building an Educated Vocabulary
Word Smart II: How to Build a More Educated
  Vocabulary
Word Smart Executive
Word Smart Genius
Writing Smart

Grammar Smart Junior
Math Smart Junior
Word Smart Junior
Writing Smart Junior

Business School Companion
College Companion
Law School Companion
Medical School Companion
Pre-Law Companion

Student Access Guide to College Admissions
Student Advantage Guide to the Best 310 Colleges
Student Advantage Guide to America's Top
  Internships
Student Advantage Guide to Business Schools
Student Advantage Guide to Law Schools
Student Advantage Guide to Medical Schools
Student Advantage Guide to Paying for College
Student Advantage Guide to Summer
Student Advantage Guide to Visiting College
  Campuses
Student Advantage Guide: Help Yourself
Student Advantage Guide: The Complete Book
  of Colleges
Student Advantage Guide: The Internship Bible
Hillel Guide to Jewish Life on Campus
International Students' Guide to the United States
The Princeton Review Guide to Your Career

**Also available on cassette from Living
Language**
Grammar Smart
Word Smart
Word Smart II

THE PRINCETON REVIEW

WRITING SMART

YOUR GUIDE TO
GREAT WRITING

By Marcia Lerner

Random House, Inc.
New York 1996
http://www.randomhouse.com

Princeton Review Publishing, L.L.C.
2315 Broadway, 3rd Floor
New York, NY 10024
E-mail: info@review.com

Acknowledgments for previously published material are found on page 176.

Lerner, Marcia.
    Writing smart: your guide to great writing/ Marcia Lerner—
    1st ed.
        p.   cm.
    ISBN 0-679-75360-5 (alk. paper) : $12.00
    1. English language—Rhetoric.   2. Report writing.
    I. Title.
    PE1478.L38   1994   808.042-dc20 94-12899 CIP

Manufactured in the United States of America

9 8 7 6 5 4

First Edition

ACKNOWLEDGMENTS

I would like to thank Hanna Fox for her help with editing, lunch, and telephone procrastination. Other stars of the telephone procrastination scene are Liz Buffa, Mike Freedman (for layout inspiration as well), Nell Goddin, Sharon Lerner, and Geoff Martz. I would also like to acknowledge Kristin Fayne-Mulroy for her tireless searching out of rights and cartoons, Chris Kensler for his editing help, and Maria Quinlan and Meher Khambata for their patience and technical expertise.

CONTENTS

INTRODUCTION

"Most people won't realize that writing is a craft. You have to take your apprenticeship in it like anything else."

—Katherine Ann Porter

The written word is one of the most effective tools available; it can convince, sell, and express emotion more eloquently than many of us can in person. This book is designed to help make your writing capable of all this, and more.

Many people feel uncomfortable writing anything they know will be read by someone else, whether it is a research paper, a letter requesting employment, or a project proposal. Good writers are not only the privileged few who read nothing but Tolstoy and sit on specially designed chairs in front of roll-top desks with pigeon holes and inkwells. Good writing is a product of hard work and organization, both of which are easily accomplished by anyone with a pen and a piece of paper.

The key components of good writing, the ones to remind yourself of whenever your writing goes off track, are clarity and honesty. Clarity is for your reader. Unless you write clearly and coherently, your reader will wander from sentence to sentence, never fully grasping your point. Honesty is for you. You will write better when you understand what you are writing. If you pretend you know something about a subject of which you are ignorant, you will be exposed. If you pretend you believe something when you don't, your writing will betray you.

This book does not focus extensively on grammar or usage, so most of our comments will address these only indirectly. For excellent grammar advice see *Grammar Smart*; for excellent usage and writing advice read Strunk and White's *The Elements of Style*.

How to Use This Book

On pages xi–xv you'll find a glossary of useful terms. You should be familiar with these terms, so you don't run across any words that surprise you.

Chapter one is an extremely brief review of basic grammar. This is not intended to provide you with an understanding or knowledge of grammar, it is there to remind you of grammar you may have once known, and to familiarize you with terms that may come up in later chapters.

Chapters two through four cover the building blocks of writing—words and how to put them together well.

The final six chapters focus on six particular types of writing. Each chapter outlines a step-by-step process, provides you with editing drills, and gives a written example. At the end of each chapter is specific formatting information that you can use for your own writing projects, and a list of recommended reading. These books include examples of the type of writing covered in the chapter, additional information on the subject, or odd writings we thought you might like.

Fiction writing will not be covered in this book, as it is an entirely different ball game (look, our first metaphor!). If you are interested in writing fiction put this book down and go find *The Art of Fiction* by John Gardner.

Writing means getting words on paper, and good writing means getting words on paper clearly. Understand that, and work hard, and you are on your way to better prose. Working through this book will improve your writing, but your instruction should not end there. The other sure way to improve your writing is to improve your reading. By providing yourself with good role models, your writing can only get better.

And that's it; you're ready to go. Read, write, and enjoy.

Glossary

The following terms appear throughout this book; you should be familiar with all of them. If you find other words in the book that you do not understand, haul out your dictionary and look them up. Using the dictionary and building vocabulary will only improve your writing. Many of the following words have more than one meaning, but the definitions provided refer only to the way they are used in this book, and should allow you to proceed easily.

ADJECTIVE: A word modifying a noun.

"*tall* tree" or "*silly* rabbit"

The words in italics are adjectives.

ADVERB: A word modifying a verb or an adjective.

"She ran *quickly*."

"The *extremely* happy clam."

The words in italics are adverbs.

BIBLIOGRAPHY: A list of reference sources, usually books.

CLAUSE: A group of words that contains a subject and a verb and can act as a modifier or a noun.

"*Anyone who likes balloons* should stay away from me."

The words in italics form a clause that is used here as a noun, and the subject of the sentence.

COLLABORATIVE WRITING: Writing done with more than one person, everyone (you hope) working together.

COLON: A punctuation mark used to indicate the amplification of a point, or a following list.

"These are the important things: food, shelter, and television."

colon

COMMA: A punctuation mark indicating a pause.

"She walked to the door, but she did not open it."

↑

comma

DOUBLE SPACE: To place the typed lines of writing an extra space apart.

ENDNOTE: A note at the end of a paper indicating the origin of a quote or idea, giving the author of the quote or idea and where it was originally published.

ESSAY: A written piece about one topic, usually fairly short.

FOOTNOTE: A note at the bottom of a page (makes sense, right?) indicating the origin of a quote or idea, giving the author of the quote or idea and where it was originally published.

INDENT: To move in the first word of a paragraph, usually five spaces.

INDEPENDENT CLAUSE: A clause that can stand by itself as a sentence.

"*Rachel laughed at the landlord,* and walked away."

The words in italics could be a whole separate sentence, they form an independent clause.

MODIFIER: A word or group of words that describes.

"*red* apple"

"*Singing on the stage,* Kelly found her *true* calling."

The words in italics are modifiers, or modifying phrases.

NOUN: A word that names something.

"*Trees* are often pleasant."

The word in italics is a noun.

OUTLINE: An organizational plan for a piece of writing.

See page 76 for an example.

PARAGRAPH: A subsection of a written work, made of one or more sentences, focused on a particular idea.

PARENTHESES: Special punctuation marks used to set a phrase off from the rest of the text.

"Many people believe (more than they really should) that Santa Claus exists."

    ↑ parenthesis   ↑ parenthesis

PHRASE: A group of words that does not contain both a subject and verb, and acts as a noun or a modifier.

"*Flying a kite* is torture for some."

In the preceding sentence, the words in italics are a noun phrase.

PRONOUN: A word that replaces a noun.

"Grace said *she* is supposed to receive the million dollars."

The word in italics is a pronoun.

PROSE: Any writing that is not poetry.

REDUNDANCY: Unnecessary repetition of a word or phrase.

"She was *completely entirely* convinced."

The words in italics have the same meaning.

RESEARCH PAPER: A paper based on research of a particular subject using a variety of outside sources.

SEMICOLON: A punctuation mark used to separate independent clauses.

"I went to the store; I hated everything there."

    ↑ semicolon

SENTENCE: A word or group of words with a subject and a verb.

SINGLE SPACE: To place typed lines of writing without any extra spaces between them.

SUBJECT: The part of a sentence that performs the action.

"*Joshua* won the lottery."

"Joshua" is the subject of the sentence.

TONE: The general quality of the atmosphere of writing, much like tone of voice.

Tone can be casual ("I'm going down to the corner store") or formal ("I am proceeding to the emporium at the edge of the avenue").

TOPIC SENTENCE: A sentence, generally at the beginning of a paragraph, that explains the main point of that paragraph.

VERB: A word expressing action or a state of being.

"Keith *plays* the electric guitar."

The word in italics is a verb.

THE PRINCETON REVIEW

WRITING SMART

YOUR GUIDE TO GREAT WRITING

The Briefest Grammar Review in the World

This review will help you brush up on some basic grammatical terms we will be using throughout this book. If you need a more thorough review, refer to the bibliography section at the end of chapter three for suggested books to assist you. You are not being asked to commit any of these terms to memory for their own sake. Remembering the terms for different points of grammar will help you on your journey toward a better understanding of clear expression.

SENTENCES

A **sentence** is a grammatical construction, containing a **subject** and an **action**, expressing an idea.

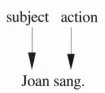

subject   action

Joan sang.

The subject of a sentence is the part that is responsible for the action, in this case "Joan." The action in this case is "sang."

Subjects are **nouns**; nouns are words that name things, such as "tree," "rock," "fish." Groups of words can act as nouns: "walking to the store" can be the subject, for instance, as in "Walking to the store sucks."

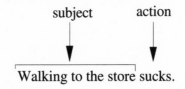

subject   action

Walking to the store sucks.

Actions are usually **verbs**; verbs are words expressing an action or a state of being. Some examples are: "jump," "be," "laugh."

PRONOUNS

Pronouns are words that replace nouns. Some of our favorite pronouns are: I, he, she, and that.

pronoun

Fred likes Joan because she is nice.

"She" is a pronoun replacing "Joan."

MODIFIERS

Modifiers are words that describe. Modifiers can be **adjectives** or **adverbs**. Adjectives describe nouns, adverbs describe either verbs or adjectives.

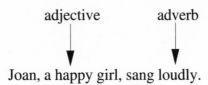

adjective   adverb

Joan, a happy girl, sang loudly.

"Happy" is an adjective modifying "girl." "Loudly" is an adverb modifying how Joan sang.

Phrases

Phrases are groups of words that act as nouns or modifiers. "Walking to the store" is a phrase, and it can be a noun phrase as it was earlier, or a modifying phrase, in which it describes something else.

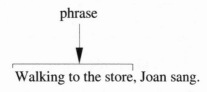

The phrase "Walking to the store" describes Joan, so it is a modifying phrase.

Clauses

Clauses are groups of words that can also act as nouns or modifiers. The only difference between a phrase and a clause is that a clause has a subject and a verb, while a phrase does not.

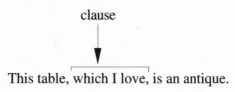

"Which I love" is the clause, and it modifies table.

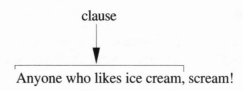

"Anyone who likes ice cream" is the clause and the subject of the sentence, so it is a noun clause.

RULES

Now, some basic rules. There are many more grammatical rules than the ones given here, but most grammatical rules exist for the sake of clarity. If you are trying to figure out which route to take, follow the one that clarifies meaning. A thorough knowledge of grammar will only improve your writing, so you are encouraged to learn as much as you can beyond these basics. These are fine as a beginning. Try to remember that memorization of the rules or labels of grammar is not your goal, a greater facility with language is.

SUBJECTS MUST AGREE WITH VERBS

If you use a singular subject, use a singular verb.

> "Joan *likes* hats." Yes.
> "Joan *like* hats." No.

If you use a plural subject, use a plural verb.

> "Joan and Fred *like* hats." Yes.
> "Joan and Fred *likes* hats." No.

PRONOUNS MUST AGREE WITH NOUNS THEY REPLACE

> "*Joan* likes the ugly hat *she* made yesterday." Yes.
> "*Joan* likes the ugly hat *they* made yesterday." No.

A PRONOUN'S REFERENCE MUST ALWAYS BE CLEAR

> "Sometimes when *Mike and Tim* go out, *they* buy beer." Yes.
> "Sometimes when *Mike and Tim* go out, *he* buys beer." No.

MODIFYING PHRASES MUST BE *NEXT TO* WHAT THEY DESCRIBE

> "*Walking to the store, Joan* was hit by a car." Yes.
> "*Walking to the store, a car* hit Joan." No.

And that's your grammar review! If you already knew everything in this chapter, you are more than ready to continue. If the information was completely new to you, why don't you read through it once more. It gets easier every time.

CHAPTER 2

Getting Ready to Write

Y ou do not just sit down and write a paper or an essay. It's not that easy. Once you have your assignment you must first get ready to write. Getting ready involves some organizing, outlining, and planning. *Then* you write. We're not saying you need to know absolutely down to the last detail how you will write about your subject before you begin writing. Often, the process of writing will help you discover exactly what you want to say, but preparation can help make your writing stronger and clearer.

RESEARCH

If your writing includes research, it is best to get a substantial chunk of the research done before you begin writing. Often information you discover as you research will alter what you might have written, so avoid endless revisions and get as much information as you can, first.

OUTLINE

If you are writing anything longer than a paragraph, it is advisable to construct an outline. An outline describes paragraph by paragraph what you intend to say; it gives you a plan for your writing, so you can chart the beginning, middle, and end of your piece. Of course, no law says that you must follow your outline down to the last detail. The process of writing can give you new ideas of what to write next, so you may want to revise your outline as you go along. Outlines will be covered in more detail in the chapter on research papers.

ENVIRONMENT

There will be a million reasons to get up once you sit down, "Oh, I need more paper, or a new pen, or a towel to wipe off my computer screen." While it is absolutely fine to take breaks when writing, jumping up every five seconds is not helpful to your momentum. Have what you need at hand, and make your surroundings pleasant enough that you might want to stay there for a few hours.

GET YOUR BUTT IN THE CHAIR

Perhaps the most difficult task is getting yourself to sit down and write. There are many techniques. Some writers bribe themselves with small treats. "If I write one page then I get to go see a movie." Others try to cast their friends as the motivating force. It is said that Ernest Hemingway actually paid his friends to force him to write two hours every morning. What we have found most effective is the worst task scenario. Say, for instance, that you have to write a book on writing. First set a reasonable schedule that will ensure your finishing, say, four hours a day. Then, if you find that when you are supposed to be sitting down, you are actually wandering the house, or gazing into the refrigerator when you are sure that you sat yourself down only a minute ago, try to bargain with yourself. Be kind. Make yourself an offer you can't refuse. Tell yourself that you have two choices, either you scrub your bathroom, or you write. In all probability you will end up with an extremely clean bathroom and a finished piece of writing. You may be forced to resort to vile threats in this sort of situation—either you visit dreaded relatives or you write the next page—but in all likelihood you will be able to find tasks far worse than writing, and so will be able to get yourself to sit down and write the thing, whatever it is.

WRITE SOMETHING DOWN

Most writing is essentially revision, and revision can only happen when there is something to revise. When you write you are much like a sculptor who must produce her own clay. Don't agonize over which clay to get, just get some. Even if you hate the first four sentences you write, often you must get them out before you can write the fifth one, which you will keep.

> "Get black on white."
>
> —Guy de Maupassant

And that's it. Once you know what your subject is and you have your materials all set up around you, don't agonize over how to begin. Simply write a sentence. Good or bad, that sentence will start you on the road to completion.

CHAPTER 3

Words, Punctuation, Sentences, and Paragraphs

To write well you must understand the function of words, sentences, paragraphs, and the way these elements work together. Words join to form sentences, sentences join to form paragraphs, and paragraphs join to become longer works, sometimes chapters, sometimes papers.

> "What can be said at all, can be said clearly."
>
> —Ludwig Wittgenstein

This chapter will provide you with some stylistic guidelines for stringing words together to form good, clear prose. The guidelines are only suggestions based on common mistakes most writers make. The basic rules of grammar will not be covered here so if you are unsure of those, buy yourself a copy of *Grammar Smart* and review. You should also be aware that many writers fearlessly break these rules and still produce fabulous, coherent writing, but unless you have an absolutely pressing reason to break one of the rules of grammar, don't.

WORDS

> "Prefer the familiar word to the far-fetched.
> Prefer the concrete to the abstract.
> Prefer the single word to the circumlocution.
> Prefer the short word to the long."
>
> —H.W. and F.G. Fowler

If you can remember these lines, your word choice will be all it is meant to be. For a somewhat more in-depth discussion, read on.

SLANG

Written English has different standards than spoken English. When you are conversing you can amplify your meaning with gestures, facial expressions, tone of voice, and word emphasis. These aids are not available to your written communication. Thus your written work must be as absolutely clear as you can make it. There may be some members of your reading audience who will be unfamiliar with colloquial uses of words such as "radical," "dude," "chill," "def," "dis," "like," "iced," etc. Unless you are going to clearly explain the use of a word in its context, do not use it in a nonstandard way.

BIG WORDS

"Henceforth I would desire to act in a more
extemporaneous manner."

equals

"I want to be more spontaneous."

The perfect word to use is the one that most nearly conveys exactly what you mean. Do not consult your thesaurus for the largest word you can squeeze into your sentence. In most cases this will make your sentence awkward and ungainly, and will give your prose a stiff and pretentious air. If the word you need is large, fine, so be it. Avoid seeking it out, is all we ask.

REPETITION

"Grace was walking her dog and then the dog
threw up and the dog was very ashamed and
sat down and would not move. Poor dog, the
dog was so sad."

One use of the thesaurus that *is* defensible is as a means to avoid excessive repetition. Certain words will be repeated in a paper or essay. If your piece is about dogs it will be difficult to avoid using the word "dog," but, when possible, avoid repetition. You can do this by looking in the thesaurus for other words that will fit. In this case, we can eliminate repetition.

"Grace was walking her dog and it vomited,
then was ashamed and would not move. Poor,
sad animal."

REDUNDANCY

Redundancy is different from repeating a necessary word or phrase, because redundancy is repeating an *unnecessary* word or phrase. "The reason why..." is a redundant phrase because if you are providing a reason for something, that already implies "why."

A few redundancies that plague writers:

BAD		BETTER
the reason is because	*say*	the reason
very unique	*say*	unique
as long or longer than	*say*	at least as long
never ever	*say*	never

Unfortunately, redundancy can crop up anywhere, not just with words but in sentences or even paragraphs. Unnecessary sentences weaken your writing. The sentences you retain can be as lush and long as you like, just make sure that each word, each sentence, and each paragraph contributes something essential to your writing. If it does not, omit it.

USAGE

TRESPASSERS
WILL BE
PERSECUTED

Oops. The sign probably meant "prosecute," and whoever wrote it didn't bother to check which word was accurate and ended up looking like a big dope. When in doubt, check your usage. If you are not certain of the word or the form of the word you are using, look it up in the dictionary. There are many words that make people unsure, and they are very simple to check. No one will ever know your ideas are brilliant if they are not well expressed.

HE OR SHE

A tough decision. Since many collective nouns are singular, you must choose something for your pronoun. For instance, the word "everyone," a collective noun, is singular. In the sentence, "Everyone has an ice cream flavor he thinks is best," you must choose a singular pronoun. The choice made in most grammar books is to use "he." "But what of feminism and equality?" you ask. Some writers use s/he to imply that while they know it is singular, either he or she thinks the ice cream flavor is best. Still others use "he or she." In the interests of brevity we believe it is better to avoid "he or she," and in the interests of verbal grace we think it is better to avoid "s/he." You may use "he" consistently; it is considered grammatically correct, though exclusionary. Desirable alternatives are to use the plural third person pronoun when possible, or to alternate between he and she, much as we are doing in this book, as long as your meaning remains clear.

AVOIDING "I"

Sometimes an author will prefer simply to describe the setting or subject of his piece without referring to himself specifically.

> "People say 'I'm having trouble with my relationship,' as though the trouble were not with Penelope or Max but with an object, like a BMW, a sort of container or psychological condition into which they enter and relate."
>
> —Leonard Michaels

Notice Mr. Michaels does not write, "I refer to my relationship" but rather "People say. . ." This allows the author to put distance between himself and what he is saying. Before you write, decide from what point of view you will write. This means you need to decide whether you want to refer to yourself in the first person singular, "I," as you would do in a personal essay, or if, like Leonard Michaels, you want to leave the "I" out of the piece altogether, or if you want to use "we" as we do in this book to make yourself sound like an ancient English ruler.

You may be writing about something from which you want to maintain a certain emotional distance—you may be writing an academic paper describing experiments you don't entirely approve of. Whatever the case may be, avoiding the first person "I" or "we" allows you to describe without necessarily putting your opinions in where they are not asked for.

Most academic papers and exams are better written with no reference to the "I" author.

USING "I"

> "I guess most people found it hard to believe that Elvis Presley didn't die after all but instead is alive and well and shopping at Felpausc's Supermarket, in Vicksburg, Michigan. I know I did when I read about it in the *New York Times* last fall."
>
> —Sue Hubbell

Using the first person can make a writer appear more intimate with her reader, and make the writing more accessible to the reader. In a personal essay for a college or graduate school, the use of the first person "I" is expected and acceptable. In more academic writing such as essays and research papers you would do best to keep yourself out of it.

USING "YOU"

Directly addressing the reader is a dicey business, only to be attempted if you are sure it is both necessary and helpful to what you are writing. It is advisable if you are writing a how-to book, as we are doing here. In any other type of writing, avoid the use of the word "you." The easiest way to do this is to leave "you" understood. Here's an example:

> "Picture two men standing on the side of the road."

It is clear the author wants *you* the reader to picture the two men, but he avoids saying "you." The other, more formal way of avoiding "you" is to use "one," as in, "One never knows what one has missed until the moment has passed." It does sound stiff, but it can be useful, particularly in academic prose in which you should *never* use "you."

CONSISTENCY

Whatever point of view you select, stick with it throughout your piece. "We think it is important that I be consistent when she writes this book." See how it can throw you off? The less opportunity the reader has to be confused or befuddled, the better off the writer is.

BEWARE YOUR VERBAL CRUTCH

Most people have a word that they use as a catch-all for a variety of meanings. These words have their uses, but you should understand what your particular crutch means to you, whether it is "weird" or "like" or "whatever." You can then search it out in your writing and clarify your meaning by examining where it appears and substituting the word you really mean. If you cannot identify your personal verbal tic, ask friends or family. Most likely they will know immediately.

MAINTAIN A WORD'S NATURAL STATE

"He really weirded me out with that peanut butter pizza." Aside from the myriad other faults in the preceding sentence, the word "weird" is used as a verb. Weird is not a verb, it is an adjective. There are enough words in the English language for you to express your meaning without bastardizing. Try instead, "I was horrified and disgusted by his peanut butter pizza."

USE THE VERB YOU INTEND

When your verbs start to become dramatic, beware. The drama of your prose should come from your thoughts, not from soppy words. If you want to say someone walked into the street and asked someone for directions, by all means say so. For instance, you probably want to avoid, "He leapt off the curb and begged for help." In most cases, the more reserved your words, the more creative your writing. Excessively dramatic words such as, "He wept, sobbed, pleaded, etc., etc.," generally have no place in well-written prose.

DON'T USE DON'T

We know, we know, it isn't fair. If we can use contractions, how come you can't? Well, when writing something formal and academic, you must try to do what your instructor wants you to do. And the rule is, avoid using contractions in academic writing. As stilted as it may sound, use "do not" instead of "don't," and so on, unless you are writing something very informal.

PUNCTUATION

> "All we can do is hang on to our colons: punctuation is bound to change, like the rest of language; punctuation is made for man, not man for punctuation; a good sentence should be intelligible without the help of punctuation in most cases; and, if you get in a muddle with your dots and dashes, you may need to simplify your thoughts, and shorten your sentence."
>
> —Phillip Howard

For standard punctuation rules, consult *Grammar Smart*. You probably know most of them anyway. It is unusual punctuation that concerns us here. We understand how tempting that top line of the key board is, above the numbers. Oh, to be able to write, "Why you dirty *#@%#!!" Unfortunately, funky punctuation more often detracts from writing than adds to it. For most prose other than fiction, you may want to leave out exclamation points entirely. Ditto the ampersand (&). Try for only a dash of dashes (sorry, we couldn't help ourselves), and restrain your use of colons (:) and semicolons (;). Effective prose writing does not call attention to itself as much as to the ideas it conveys. Of course, with punctuation, as with any other part of writing, once you have learned the rules you are free to wreak havoc with them. Just try to ensure that any havoc you wreak is justified, so that once the noise and thrill of fifteen ampersands, ten dashes and twenty-five exclamation points in one sentence has worn off, there is something in the sentence left to consider.

SENTENCES

> "Take care to avoid getting asked the favorite question of Harold Ross, *The New Yorker's* late editor: 'What the hell do you mean?'"
>
> —Kathleen Krull

Good sentences communicate a point clearly. When writing a sentence, it is helpful to ask yourself, "Does it say exactly what I mean?" Form what you want to say in your head, then write that down. If your meaning is obscured, your sentence needs to be trimmed or entirely rewritten. Often the most beautiful writing is the simplest. So, keep it simple.

The following guidelines will help you achieve greater clarity, but do not expect to write perfect sentences every time. Much of this advice will be useful in the rewriting and editing processes covered in the next chapter.

VARY SENTENCE STRUCTURE
Sentences can start with their subjects, as this one just did. Or they can start with conjunctions, like this sentence. Using the same structure, sentence after sentence, can give your prose a droning quality which you probably want to avoid. So do.

MAINTAIN REASONABLE EXPECTATIONS OF YOUR SENTENCES
Most sentences convey one or two images. Don't overload your sentence with a freight too heavy for it to bear by adding comma after comma and phrase after phrase. You can always extend your metaphor or story or paragraph by adding sentences. Long sentences are difficult to control, so stick to manageable lengths. It is also easier to identify and repair flaws in shorter sentences.

"I want to go to college and become more educated, because education is very important, and the economy is calling for people who have rigorous scholastic training." Yikes. Way too much.

"I want to go to college to become more educated. Education is very important, and the economy is calling for people with rigorous scholastic training." Better.

USE THE ACTIVE VOICE

"I bought a bagel."

or

"A bagel was bought by me."

The first is active, the second is passive. Whenever possible, use the active. Active is more concise, cogent, and appealing than passive; overall it is simply more effective.

HUMOR

While almost all writing can benefit from humor, a humorous tone is very difficult to master. Your reader won't know the exact timing and inflection that your sentence relies on; it must be able to stand alone. One way of checking tone is to read aloud what you have written, using as little vocal inflection as possible. If your sentence is still funny, congratulations. If without inflection it is no longer funny, cut it.

DESCRIPTION

Description is an incredibly helpful tool in writing. It allows the writer to show more clearly what he intended.

Nick included this sentence in an essay on his college application. He is describing his employment in an effort to communicate to the admissions officer that because of his particular job, he has experience that will make him an outstanding candidate. Here is the sentence:

I work.

As the reader of this sentence, do you clearly understand what Nick is trying to communicate? Not really, and neither would the admissions counselor. How about:

I work at the ice cream parlor.

Now you know more about Nick because he has altered his sentence to express more specifically what he is trying to communicate. Even so, if this is to be his introductory sentence, a sentence that includes more information may be appropriate:

> I work at the ice cream parlor near my house,
> and my job has taught me much about my
> neighbors.

But beware, while clear communication is essential, over-describing by tacking on description after description will muddy the prose and render the focus of the sentence unclear.

> I work at the ice cream parlor near my house,
> which is in a low grey building made of old
> crumbling cinder block piled high and ominous
> against the mostly grey skies you find in Boston
> in November, and my job has taught me much
> about my neighbors.

Nick may walk away from that sentence patting himself on the back for his moving and descriptive turns of phrase, but as the reader you get an entirely different message from the previous sentence. Too much description ends up weakening the entire sentence. Does he enjoy his work? Is that the point? Or is the ice cream parlor a depressing place? Or is his house? Unless you intend to use contradictions to enhance a sentence's meaning, avoid them.

UNDERSTAND METAPHOR, BUT USE IT SPARINGLY

> "Once at least in the life of every human, whether
> he be brute or trembling daffodil, comes a
> moment of complete gastronomic satisfaction."
>
> —M.F.K. Fisher

A metaphor is a word or image used to describe something not like itself, for instance: "A human is a trembling daffodil."

A metaphor is one of the most effective weapons in your arsenal. "A weapon?" you say. Ah, we were speaking metaphorically. Equating a word such as "weapon" to another is using metaphor. "That test was a piece of cake" is another metaphor. An extended metaphor lasts beyond the one image and can go on for sentences, or even paragraphs.

Extended metaphors are a difficult enterprise and are probably best avoided until you are more comfortable. Don't use a metaphor unless you feel that the thing you are describing could be better described in no other way. Otherwise you will end up saying, "The car was a tiger running over the plains in the jungle," when it would have been far clearer to say what you may have meant, "The car was fast and sleek." Also avoid mixing metaphors. A mixed metaphor starts out with one image and ends with another: "That test was a piece of cake and it was smooth sailing all the way." The reader is left to wonder, "Which is it? The test was the cake or the water?" When a reader is confused her attention wanders, and you have lost her.

UNDERSTAND SIMILE, BUT USE IT SPARINGLY

> "As alarming as the Gaines-burgers were, their soy-meal began to seem like an old friend when the time came to try some *canned* dog foods."
>
> —Ann Hodgman

Ms. Hodgman refers here to soy-meal seeming like an old friend, a perfect example of simile. A simile resembles a metaphor, but it uses the word "like." A simile also uses something other than what is being described to describe it. "An old friend" to describe "soy-meal." Like other descriptive methods, simile should only be used when necessary to your sentence.

IMAGES

"Viewed from a suitable height, the aggregating clusters of medical scientists in the bright sunlight of the boardwalk in Atlantic City, swarmed there from everywhere for the annual meetings, have the look of assemblages of social insects."

—Lewis Thomas

As we will probably say a billion more times, good writing is clear writing. One of the great ways to make writing clear is to provide a clear image, a physical example for the reader to see. Whether it is a metaphor, as here, or a visual picture, a smell, a sound, or a taste, the more you can set the scene the easier it will be for your reader to follow you.

RHETORICAL QUESTIONS

"Where have all the thighs gone? Where are the thighs of yesteryear? This is not exactly a litany raised by many, but the heartfelt concern of a few. In recent memory I do not believe that I have entered a restaurant where thighs are allowed to stand alone proudly by themselves. I mean chicken thighs, though duck and turkey thighs are also lonely and neglected."

—Jim Harrison

A rhetorical question is a question designed to stir up thought, and is not necessarily intended to be answered.

What is the use of a rhetorical question? Well, it can help you get your reader thinking about what is going through your mind. It can also help the reader to ask the question of himself, the question to which you will then thoughtfully provide the answer. With this tool, as with all other writing tools, comes a warning:

DANGER!
Too many rhetorical questions
can induce in the reader
the strong desire to smack
the writer and tell him to
get to the damn point, already.

QUOTATIONS

Quotations can be helpful when you are looking for something snazzy to spice up your writing; just be careful not to overdo it. Unless your last name is Bartlett, there should always be more of your writing in a paper than anyone else's. Don't quote for the sake of quoting, quote because someone has said something integral to your piece of writing, and has said it far better than you can.

BE GRAMMATICAL

Follow the rules of grammar. Of course there are many great writers who have broken grammatical rules, but this does not mean that everyone can break these rules. The limitations, as annoying as they may be, are there to aid you in your attempts at clear communication. Only after you have successfully mastered them and their use should you feel free to experiment.

PARAGRAPHS

Once you have sentences, you can form paragraphs. Paragraphs are the units that make up any kind of paper or prose piece. Generally, each paragraph expresses a separate thought or idea. Paragraphs make reading easier, like cutting a steak into pieces to eat it, rather than trying to cram the whole thing into your mouth. Bear that image in mind both when you write and when you revise. You will probably write in paragraph form, but even more you will revise with paragraph form in mind.

There is no set size for a paragraph; a paragraph can be one sentence, or even a one-word sentence, for drama.

See?

A short paragraph like that can effectively highlight a point, or stop readers in their tracks to consider something. Paragraphs can also be several pages long—just read some James Joyce. As long as you try to paragraph in such a way as to convey your ideas clearly, you need not worry about the "proper" length.

Paragraphs can be set off by indentation or by double spacing. Either is acceptable, though indentation is the standard in most prose, and double spacing is generally relegated to letter formats.

Paragraphs need some transition. Arrange your paragraphs so each one leads at least semi-logically to the next. If you are going to start an entirely new thought that has no clear relation to the previous paragraph, you may want to both indent and double space, or start a new chapter if that sort of division is appropriate.

FINALLY...

Words, sentences, and paragraphs are the elements of writing. If you are having trouble expressing yourself on paper look to these components for help. Comfort and ease with these elements will improve your writing and sharpen your communication skills.

BOOK LIST

The Staff of the Princeton Review, *Grammar Smart*, Villard.

Longman, *Roget's Thesaurus of Words and Phrases*, Random House.

William Strunk and E. B. White, *The Elements of Style*, Macmillan.

CHAPTER 4

Editing

Once you have a rough draft you are only part-way through your writing process. Editing is the main work in writing excellent prose. Editing can be a painful process, eliminating words, sentences, even whole paragraphs. But, as with physical exercise, once the painful process has been completed, the results are well worth it. Besides, the results of editing, unlike the results of exercise, last.

When editing, try to read your work with an objective eye. You don't need to remind yourself how hard you worked on a particular paragraph or image, you need to decide what should be done with a particular paragraph or image *as it relates to the whole of what you are writing*. You are trying to refine the whole piece. All concerns other than the piece need to be ignored. You must stomp out that unhelpful part of your ego ("but that image is great, even if it doesn't work in this dumb paper I can't lose it"), and smother lazy urges ("but I don't wanna change it, it's good enough as is"). Make sure to allow yourself as much time as possible for this process; it is not the most pleasant for the majority of writers, and you may need to fortify yourself with frequent breaks for cookies and riveting daytime television dramas.

The editing marks you use should be easy for you to understand when you go back. If you see just a big circle with an arrow pointing out of it you may not know what you intended, so try to be clear with your remarks. There are some set forms for editing marks that we will use in the editing exercises throughout this book. This does not mean you have to use these yourself; it means you can check back here when you are trying to figure out what the heck a little squiggle might mean.

Proofreader's Marks
OPERATIONAL AND TYPOGRAPHICAL SIGNS

Mark	Meaning	Mark	Meaning
ℐ	Delete	*ital*	Set in *italic* type
◯	Close up; delete space	*rom*	Set in roman type
ℐ (closed)	Delete and close up (use only when deleting letters *within* a word)	*bf*	Set in **boldface** type
stet	Let it stand	*lc*	Set in lowercase (uncapitalized)
#	Insert space	*cap*	Set in CAPITAL letters
eq #	Make space between words equal; make leading between lines equal	*sc*	Set in SMALL CAPITALS
		wf	Wrong font; set in correct type
hr #	Insert hair space	✗	Reset broken letter
ls	Letterspace	∨	Insert here *or* make superscript (N²)
¶	Begin new paragraph	∧	Insert here *or* make subscript (N₁)
□	Move type one em from left or right		**PUNCTUATION MARKS**
⊐	Move right	⌄ (comma)	Insert comma
⊏	Move left	⌄ (apostrophe)	Insert apostrophe (or single quotation mark)
⊐⊏	Center		Insert quotation marks
⊓	Move up	⨀	Insert period
⊔	Move down	(stet) ?	Insert question mark
fl	Flush left	;/	Insert semicolon
fr	Flush right	:/	Insert colon
=	Straighten type; align horizontally	|=|	Insert hyphen
||	Align vertically	1/M	Insert em dash
tr	Transpose	1/N	Insert en dash
(sp)	Spell out	(|)	Insert parentheses

Editing usually takes place in at least three rounds. The first round consists of organizational editing.

Round One

Organization of a paper allows that paper to be read and understood logically. Much of editing lies not only in particular words or sentences but in whole paragraphs and sections of text. This is particularly true of longer pieces. On your first editing read-through of a longer piece, look for larger organizational flaws.

IS YOUR STRUCTURE SOUND?

Often your writing will seem particularly clear to you, when you are in fact missing important transitions or referring to a paragraph that doesn't come for another three pages. To avoid these problems you need to spend some time at the rough draft stage of your paper. This is when you have everything you are going to include in the paper already written, but you haven't yet read through it for spelling or smoothness, nor have you (most likely) added footnotes or other references. Before you go on to more fine-tuned sorts of editing, you need to make sure that your structure is sound.

First, read through the paper. Is it logical? Does everything seem to be in the proper order? Take notes as you read, indicating parts that seem unclear. Then divide your paper into sections. If your paper sets forth an opinion or argument, read through and separate it into the pieces of evidence that support your point. If your paper is a descriptive piece, separate it into the separate facets of your subject.

GOT A SCISSORS?

When we say divide it, we mean literally cut the paper with scissors. Compositions written in longhand or on a typewriter should be photocopied, works composed on the computer should be printed out as hard copies. Once you have separated your paper into pieces, spread them out and see if you can organize them into a more coherent whole. Experiment a bit here. Sometimes a paragraph that previously seemed dull and sad will take on a whole new life when it begins the body of a paper. Conversely, a paragraph that you had grown attached to can be exposed in this process as a nasty little parasite that is weakening the whole structure and coherence of your piece. Try many different setups, and keep a record of the ones that work best. It may be helpful here to make several copies and paste together your three best attempts at organization. You can also have other people read the paper at this stage, when it is strung together in a daring new way. Your friends or teachers can let you know whether you are being daring or just disorganized.

QUESTIONS TO ASK YOURSELF IN THE FIRST ROUND OF EDITS

Is this the logical way I would argue this point if I were talking to someone?
If you wouldn't talk this way on your best arguing day, there is probably a better way to organize it. Often ideas will come to you as you are writing and you will include them as you think of them. This is all well and good but it probably means that they are somewhat out of order. Once you have a rough draft of your piece, look at all the evidence and information you include. You can even put the subject of each paragraph on a note card, then move them around on the desk until they are well ordered. It will help to listen to someone who builds up logically to a point, so read some magazine articles in a well-written magazine, such as *Harper's*, *The Atlantic Monthly*, or *The Nation*. Articles in these magazines string evidence together and come up with conclusions.

Does each paragraph proceed smoothly from the previous one?
This has much to do with the last and first sentences of paragraphs. Readers know that when a new paragraph begins they should expect a somewhat new thought, but they also expect it to relate in some way to the thoughts just expressed. If there is no immediate connection, either create an entirely new section, not just a new paragraph, or write a transition sentence to begin the new paragraph. This transition sentence performs basically the same function as a comedian's transition, "So, speaking of kangaroos, I was talking to an Australian guy the other day. . . ." It allows the audience to follow a logical train and not lose sight of the path the performer is taking. You can still allow your reader to make some deductions, but don't force him to guess how things fit.

Are related paragraphs near each other?
If you refer to a dog named Gary in one paragraph, then refer to the dog again later as just "Gary," you need to ascertain that the

reader knows to whom or to what you are referring. This can be a particular danger if you have moved paragraphs around in the editing process.

Does each paragraph explain itself well to the reader, or does it rely on additional knowledge that should also be included? Even though you will often be writing for an instructor, do not assume that your instructor already knows exactly what you are referring to when you write, "After the war there was a lot of trouble for everyone cleaning up." Which war? All the subjects in your paper should be introduced with clarity.

ROUND TWO

When you have a structure you are comfortable with, you are ready for the next stage: editing for style.

> "[What to do when a sentence stinks]: Change it. How? Easy. Read a stinky sentence over. Figure out what it means. Now . . . put the sentence's meaning in your own words. . . . You may have to expand the sentence into two or three sentences. That's allowed."
>
> —Bill Scott

EDITING FOR STYLE

You will probably notice some awkward sentences as you go through the reorganizing round. Now you will return and look for them mercilessly. If you are using pen and paper or a typewriter to compose, put these changes onto the pasted-together rough draft from your first round of edits. If you are using the computer, you will have already pasted together a version in the computer. It is probably helpful to print out that new version and put your edits on the hard copy. You can then enter them once you have gone through this second round.

When writing, try to get as much down as possible, but when editing, make sure that each piece is serving its appropriate function in its appropriate place.

Introductory sentences must be both welcoming and precise. At the beginning of a paragraph, a paper, or an essay, you must try to open the door (yes, that's a metaphor) for your reader so she will look inside and want to enter. Whatever type of paper you are writing, you are creating a world that the reader will enter, even if only for a few sentences. Your opening sentence should orient your reader so she knows what you will be talking about and from what point of view. For the other sentences, since you have already checked your paper for logical soundness, you are now seeing whether your writing clearly communicates your logic. Scrutinize each sentence. Poke. Prod. If you find a sentence that doesn't work, rewrite it. If it still doesn't work after one or two rewrites, start a new sentence from scratch. It is easier to create anew than to fix something rotten to the core. You should also check for spelling, grammar, and punctuation here. Keep a dictionary and a copy of *The Chicago Manual of Style* on hand to check these fine points.

QUESTIONS TO ASK YOURSELF IN THE SECOND ROUND

Does this sentence convey its idea clearly?
When you were writing you knew what you meant, but will the reader know? "I felt as I always do when I hear Rachmaninoff," may mean you were frightened, exhilarated, or infuriated, but your reader will be unable to understand unless you open your private world of images to her. When you edit, think of this reader, and how each word, sentence, and paragraph would seem to her.

Does each sentence flow from the previous one?
Paragraphs should form coherent wholes. If there is too large a jump from sentence to sentence the reader will become confused and lose the train of thought you have established.

Are any sentences unnecessary to the whole?
Extraneous sentences can bore a reader faster than anything else. In general, if within one paragraph you find two sentences that say the same thing, one of them can go. Of course, in certain circumstances repetition can be used for dramatic emphasis, and this is where you

can again ask yourself, "Is this sentence necessary to the whole?" If not, strike it out.

Are any words unnecessary to the whole?
Redundancy is lethal to good style; avoid unnecessary words.

Is the point of view consistent?
Refer to the point of view section in the previous chapter, pages 17–18. You should use only one point of view throughout a piece.

Is the tense consistent?
Use the simple past tense for most academic writing. There will be exceptions, particularly when referring to various historical events that occurred at different points in time, but for clarity's sake, be consistent in your use of tenses.

Does this sentence say *exactly* what I mean?
You had a particular point you wanted to get across within each sentence you wrote. Does the sentence say what you meant? Check to see if a certain word could be fine-tuned to be more exact. "I wanted to take a walk before it got too dark" is not the same thing as, "I was afraid it would soon be too dark for me to walk safely." The first is matter-of-fact and slightly impatient, while the second implies a certain amount of trepidation, nervousness, and hesitation.

Is this sentence true?
This relates more to honesty in writing. Before you allow a sentence like, "The lightning flashed and a tree shuddered next to me, but I was not afraid," make sure that it is either literally true, or a very well-planned bit of misinformation, leading to humor or the like.

Is there a variety of sentence structure in this paragraph?
While a certain amount of sentence structure repetition can lend your writing a particular rhythm, the same sentence structure over and over will cause your readers to tear their hair out by the roots. If you see five sentences in a row beginning the same way, with "if" or an "ing" word, see if you can transform a few of them.

Is each pronoun in this sentence necessary?
We are all subject to the late-twentieth-century plague of unnecessary

pronouns. Chief among the culprits are "that," "which," and "it." When you see any one of this unholy trio, try the sentence without it. Does it still work? If so, eliminate the pronoun.

Does each pronoun refer to something the reader can understand?
You may find sentences that seem perfectly intelligible but have a mysterious floating pronoun. "It is very difficult to understand why there is violence in this world." The first "it" has no clear reference, and "this" preceding "world" makes it seem as though the writer has had some experience on other worlds, as does bringing up "the world" at all. Where else could the author refer to? "The existence of violence is incomprehensible" is a more concise way of expressing the same idea.

Is the sentence grammatically correct?
Take no chances here. If you are unsure, consult a book. While you can amend spelling mistakes, typos, and punctuation in the last round of editing (though you will have caught most mistakes by then), grammatical errors too often demand a reconstruction of the sentence. This reconstruction is too messy to appear on the final version of a paper, so attend to it now.

Do I avoid the passive voice?
That sounds much better than, "Has the passive voice been avoided by me?" doesn't it? When possible, sentences should be in the active voice. If you have a long, unruly, or dragging sentence, passive voice may well be the problem.

Does my verbal crutch appear anywhere?
Those of you who have computers will have a much easier time here. You can simply have your computer search for whatever your phrase is, if you know what you are in the habit of saying. A student of ours always searches for "weird," "annoying," and "most people believe," because he has been told that these words and phrases crop up more often than is healthy in his writing. An appearance once or twice is fine, six times in one chapter goes over the top. If you don't have a computer, just try to stay vigilant. Be on the lookout for any word or phrase that appears multiple times.

Do I have clichéd images?
Dark as night, bright like the sun, like a pack of vicious animals, on and on the cliché march goes. A cliché is an image that has been used so much and so often that it has actually been worn out. Readers are so used to seeing clichés that whatever power the image or saying once had is dismissed by the reader. Comb your writing for clichés. Whenever you see a phrase you recognize as overly familiar, strike it out.

Have I gone crazy with adverbs, adjectives, and other description?
Adverbs, along with most forms of description, should be used sparingly. Description should suggest, not give every detail. Readers resent being bullied. Present your readers with an image, don't smash their faces in it.

Do I sound like myself?
You should sound like yourself. Attempts to sound otherwise, either more correct or, heaven help you, writerly, will only misrepresent you and stilt your writing.

Is there stylistic closure?
Closure ties together loose ends and allows readers to feel they have truly finished, instead of being cut off in some premature way. Most writing requires some sort of conclusion to provide closure. A conclusion can be any length, depending on the length of your piece. Symmetry may serve as an effective stylistical tool in creating closure. If you begin your paper with an anecdote, ending with an anecdote can be beautifully symmetrical. This also works if you begin with a quotation, a theory, or an historical reference. Consistency of example allows you to give your readers a feeling of satisfaction when they have reached the end of your paper. No matter how you accomplish it, closure is why a conclusion is necessary to most writing.

ROUND THREE

Before you go through your piece this final time, you must enter your second round of edits. Computer users can enter these on the copy in the computer, pen and typewriter users will have to write up another draft.

IN THE THIRD ROUND, PROOFREAD

Proofreading is your opportunity to indulge that nit-picking streak you have kept hidden from the world. Or, this may be your opportunity to develop that streak. In the third round of editing you are looking for the tiny little errors that are floating around your almost entirely cleaned-up manuscript. You are checking things you have already checked, like spelling, punctuation, typos, indentations, numbering on pages, underlining or italicization of titles (italics are preferable if you have them), and capitalization of proper names. If you are writing on a computer you have the benefit of the spell check, though a spell check is not enough on its own, because it does not repair words to form other, correctly spelled words—"form" to "from," for example. So be extra careful and proofread for spelling anyway. For the rest of you, when in doubt, look it up in the dictionary. For points other than spelling, keep that copy of *The Chicago Manual of Style* or the *MLA Handbook* with you, and mercilessly check all fine points.

Once you have checked all these points give your paper a visual going over. Erase any nasty marks, or use white out. Get yourself one of those lovely paper binders in a nice celluloid pink (you don't actually have to do this but it could be fun), and you are ready to go.

Editing Drill Number One

The following paragraph is part of a research paper discussing commercial novels of the 1980s, and has many organizational and stylistic problems; nothing fatal, but you should attempt to identify these problems by editing the paragraph. Try to address the questions brought up in the editing rounds we just discussed, though in this case you will have to edit all in one round. Feel free to look back at previous chapters. When you are done compare the edits you made with the edits made on the following page, and see how they differ. If our edits don't correspond exactly with yours, don't be alarmed. Everyone edits in a different way, and your own personal style will have much to do with the words you choose to leave in or take out. After you have compared the two, look at the final version in which all the edits have been made. Are they what you would have done? Can you see how the paragraph has been improved? When you edit, remember that this paragraph is part of a research paper and should have an academic tone.

Some of the foremost examples of the trash novels of the eighties are those written by Jackie Collins and Judith Krantz. These novels mention in tiny meticulous detail all the money and the merchandise that money can procure, that belongs to their usually female characters. Thus, money becomes a dream of the woman of the nineteen eighties. This is not to say that these role models were only about money. Not only the money but what many of these novelists almost equated with money; fabulous looks and torrid romances. In Scruples, the tons of money, excessive pulchritude, and boundless ambition of the main character only convince you further of my point: so-called trash novels are attempts by women, for women, to cast themselves into a more positive fantasy than the one offered by other media, namely television and films of the same time.

Our Version, With Edits

most popular   *unnecessary*

redundant

passive voice instead of active

wrong word, maybe "describe"

"money" repeated too many times

what is this? a book? why no italics or author?

too casual

Some of the foremost examples of the trash novels of the eighties are those written by Jackie Collins and Judith Krantz. These novels mention in tiny meticulous detail all the money and the merchandise that money can procure, that belongs to their usually female characters. Thus, money becomes a dream of the woman of the nineteen eighties. This is not to say that these role models were only about money. Not only the money but what many of these novelists almost equated with money; fabulous looks and torrid romances. In Scruples, the tons of money, excessive pulchritude, and boundless ambition of the main character only convince you further of my point: so-called trash novels are attempts by women, for women, to cast themselves into a more positive fantasy than the one offered by other media, namely television and films of the same time.

redundant

repeating word—also, does not make sense... re-write sentence.

not a full sentence

no need for fancy word, "beauty" ok

academic paper, no "you" or "me"

whole last sentence is main point— belongs at beginning

unnecessary   *unnecessary*

Final Version

The so-called trash novels of the eighties are attempts by women, for women, to cast themselves in more positive fantasy roles than those offered by other media. Jackie Collins and Judith Krantz wrote some of the most popular trash novels, which describe in meticulous detail the sumptuous financial situations of their heroines. Thus, these novels present financial stability as a dream of the woman of the nineteen eighties. This is not to say that these role models were strictly mercenary. In these novels not only money, but what many of the novelists almost always equated with money—fabulous looks and torrid romances—represent the fantasies of women of the eighties. In *Scruples*, a novel by Judith Krantz, the money, beauty, and boundless ambition of the main character further demonstrate this point.

Editing Drill Number Two

The following is a personal essay in response to this question:

> "Please provide us with a one-page summary
> of personal and family background. Include
> information on where you grew up, parents'
> occupations, any siblings, and perhaps a high-
> light or special memory of your youth."

Edit this essay for organization and style. Keep in mind the editing questions listed previously, and that this is a personal essay, and thus aims for a personal tone. Feel free to look back at this and previous chapters. On the pages following this, check the way we have edited this essay. While you should not worry if your edits are not exactly the same as ours, as there are many different ways to write, do try to determine the differences in the edits. And don't worry about the psychotic content: it's out of your hands.

When you are done comparing the two drafts, look to the final version to see how the edits were accommodated.

I grew up in New Orleans with my father, my mother, and my two brothers. When I think back of how I decided to apply to business school, I am reminded of one of my earliest childhood memories: burning ants.

I was given a camping knife for my seventh birthday, and the camping knife had many wonderful attachments, one of which was a magnifying glass. We had studied prisms and the way they focus and diffract light that year in science class, and I used my magnifying glass to cook up paper and onion grass. I burned holes in washcloths and I seared apples. But it never occurred to me to turn it on another living being: there was no reason to do so. Thus, I was a novice at killing with a magnifying glass until June 24, 1976.

My family and I were on a picnic in the park that was down the street from where we lived, celebrating the beginning of summer. My mother had brought cold roast chicken and lemonade, potato salad and fresh baked cookies. We had a wonderful time, my brothers and I played in the tall grass while the sun shone and the breeze cooled us. Everything was completely and totally fine until we sat down to eat.

Ants had come to share our picnic bounty. Not only had the ants come, but the ones that had come, they came specifically to me. They were the ones that swarmed over my plate, into my glass of lemonade, on top of my cookies. The food was then eaten by the rest of my family and laughed, while my stores of food were seen by me to be dwindling. "Can I have some of your food, mother?" I asked. "Sorry sweetie," she said, "I made enough for everyone to have an equal amount. There's no extra." I asked the others; no one would oblige me. It was the eleventh hour for me; I had to do something.

It was the ants versus me in a battle over my sustenance. Suddenly, I knew what I had to do.

I got out my camping knife and started to burn; I massacred hundreds of ants because I finally realized it was them or me. Once all the ants were either dead, wounded, or in swift retreat, I relaxed and ate my food, confident that I was strong enough to prevail over any opposition. I knew at once what my future would bring; business school.

It was then, with this first taste of the blood of my enemies, that I recognized the business school was a viable future for me. I knew I had the instinct to survive and beyond survival, thriving. My battle with the ants which had been a microcosmic antecedent to future confrontations, in which I would understand what was at stake and would win. I know this perspective and this past will help me in both business school, and my career as a managerial executive.

Our Version, With Edits

too wordy, use "consider why"

wordy—"parents"

obvious, unnecessar[y]

I grew up in New Orleans with my father, my mother, and my two brothers. When I think back of how I decided to apply to business school, I am reminded of one of my

a
earliest childhood memories: burning ants.

wordy

use "I," stick with one point of view

I was given a camping knife for my seventh birthday, and the camping knife had many wonderful attachments, one of which was a magnifying glass. We had studied prisms and the way they focus and diffract light that year in science class, and I used my magnifying glass to cook up paper and onion grass. I burned holes in washcloths and I seared apples. But it never occurred to me to turn it on

connect sentences, all one idea

use age, not year—no reason for year

another living being: there was no reason to do so. Thus, I was a novice at killing with a magnifying glass until June 24, 1976.

My family and I were on a picnic in the park that was down the street from where we lived, celebrating the beginning of summer. My mother had brought cold roast chicken and lemonade, potato salad and fresh baked cookies. We had a wonderful time, my brothers and I played in the tall grass while the sun shone and the breeze cooled us. Everything was completely and totally fine until we sat down to eat.

unnecessar[y]

start new paragraph

redundant and unnecessar[y]

extra pronouns, unnecessary

Ants had come to share our picnic bounty. Not only had the ants come, but the ones that had come, they came specifically to me. They were the ones that swarmed over my plate, into my glass of lemonade, on top of my cookies.

unnecessar[y]

passive voice, use active! — The food was then eaten by the rest of my family and I laughed, while my stores of food were seen by me to be

dwindling. "Can I have some of your food, mother?" I asked.

"Sorry sweetie," she said, "I made enough for everyone to have

an equal amount. There's no extra." I asked the others; no one

cliché — would oblige me. It was the eleventh hour for me; I had to do

something.

It was the ants versus me in a battle over my sustenance.

Suddenly, I knew what I had to do.   *sentences repeat same idea, redundant*

I got out my camping knife and started to burn; I massacred

unnecessary — hundreds of ants because I finally realized it was them or me.

Once all the ants were either dead, wounded, or in swift retreat,

I relaxed and ate my food, confident that I was strong enough to

prevail over any opposition. I knew at once what my future   *not true, I didn't know then at the picnic, too melodramatic*

add "first began to" to balance the sentence — would bring; business school.

It was then, with this first taste of the blood of my enemies,

that I recognized the business school was a viable future for me.   *too wordy, use "not only to survive but also to thrive" —or "survive, thrive, and dominate"*

I knew I had the instinct to survive and beyond survival,

too fancy— use "an omen of" — thriving. My battle with the ants which had been a microcosmic

antecedent to future confrontations, in which I would

understand what was at stake and would win. I know this

need to say "fight" before we get to "win" — perspective and this past will help me in both business school,

and my career as a managerial executive.

Final Version, With Edits Made

I grew up in New Orleans with my parents and my two brothers. When I consider why I decided to apply to business school, I am reminded of a childhood memory: burning ants.

For my seventh birthday I was given a camping knife with many wonderful attachments, one of which was a magnifying glass. I had studied prisms and the way they focus and diffract light that year in science class, and I used my magnifying glass to cook up paper and onion grass, to burn holes in washcloths and sear apples. But it never occurred to me to turn it on another living being: there was no reason to do so. Thus, I was a novice at killing with a magnifying glass until a June day when I was ten years old.

My family and I were on a picnic in the park, celebrating the beginning of summer. My mother had brought cold roast chicken, lemonade, potato salad, and fresh baked cookies. We had a wonderful time. My brothers and I played in the tall grass while the sun shone and the breeze cooled us. Everything was fine until we sat down to eat.

Ants had come to share our picnic bounty. Not only had the ants come, but they had come specifically to me. They swarmed over my plate, into my glass of lemonade, on top of my cookies. The rest of the family ate and laughed, while I saw my stores of food dwindling. "Can I have some of your food, mother?" I asked. "Sorry sweetie," she said, "I made enough for everyone to have an equal amount. There's no extra." I asked the others; no one would oblige me.

It was the ants versus me in a battle over my sustenance. Suddenly, I knew what I had to do.

I got out my camping knife, opened to the magifying lense, and started to burn; I massacred hundreds of ants because I finally realized it was them or me. Once all the ants were dead, wounded, or in swift retreat, I relaxed and ate my food, confident that I was strong enough to prevail over any opposition.

It was then, with this first taste of the blood of my enemies, that I began to recognize that business school was a viable future for me. I knew I had the instinct to survive, thrive, and dominate. My battle with the ants was an omen of future confrontations in which I would understand what was at stake, fight for it, and win. I know that this perspective and this past will help me in both business school and my career as a managerial executive.

FINALLY

There are some people who benefit from more than three drafts of a paper. You must become accustomed to your own ways of writing to determine if you are one of these. There is a person who does not need three drafts, but his name is Mozart, and he's dead. Don't confuse yourself with him.

BOOK LIST

The Chicago Manual of Style, The University of Chicago Press.

William Strunk and E. B. White, *The Elements of Style*, Macmillan.

Miss Thistlebottom's Hobgoblins: The Careful Writer's Guide to the Taboos, Bugbears, and Outmoded Rules of English Usage, Farrar, Straus, and Giroux.

CHAPTER 5

Personal
Essays

A college or graduate school asks you to write a personal essay to find out more about who you are and how you think. This is particularly true of essays that simply ask one of those horrifyingly vague questions like, "Tell us more about yourself in the space provided," or, "Describe an experience that has shaped you." The terrific thing about personal essays is that they give you the opportunity to write about something that interests you: yourself. Now don't get all indignant, we're not trying to say you are particularly self-centered, but the truth is most people take a healthy interest in what they do, otherwise, why would they do it? And generally, people write best when they are discussing something that interests them.

FORMAT

The general structure of a personal essay will vary slightly with its proposed length, but will follow this basic form: Introduction, Three Examples, Conclusion.

• **Introduction**: Your introduction will state the point you wish to make, and set up the way you will make your point. This means that before you start writing your introduction, you must know what you intend to say.

• **Examples**: The three examples should each be a separate paragraph, and should provide clear tangible evidence to support your introductory claim. For instance, if you start out saying, "I realized in the middle of last summer that I enjoy fishing," your examples must demonstrate this with some clarity: "In July I went to visit my mother in Alaska where we fished for halibut in the inland waterway." Also remember that you can have a strong point of view in a personal essay. If you enjoy hunting and fishing and feel this says something about you, don't be afraid to express your enjoyment through description. "The salt smell and the stillness of the water thrilled us, and as the day wore on we were astonished to see whales surfacing and eagles skimming the waves, all before I felt the first exciting tug on my line." Your examples can bring up subtleties of the main point you posited in your introduction. They should fill in the main point as though the main point were an outline in a coloring book and the examples were the crayons used to color it in and make it vibrant and exciting for the viewer.

• **Conclusion**: The conclusion should basically restate, in different words, the main point you presented in the introduction. You may also use this last paragraph to tie in the examples you used through the middle of your essay. Because of this, your conclusion will usually resonate more than your introduction. If the introduction is the outline and the examples color it in, the conclusion gives your work of art its title, taking into account both its shape and its color.

HOW TO WRITE IT, WITH YOUR HOST NICK

STEP 1: FOCUS ON WHAT YOU WANT TO SAY

> "A writer should concern himself with whatever absorbs his fancy, stirs his heart, and unlimbers his typewriter."
>
> —E. B. White

One of the most difficult aspects of a personal essay is its tight limitation on space. Respond to this curtailment by having a very focused thesis for your essay. This thesis should present you to your advantage. Applying to school is competitive, and you are responsible for the image you present. Your job is to enlighten the admissions committee about your wonderful qualities. No one else will do this for you. Since most personal essay questions are generalized and free-form, you may want to jot down a few things that are important to you and stew over them for a bit. Think about what you want to present to the admissions committee as your most winning character trait.

> Nick is applying to colleges, among them Harvard. Here is the question he must confront. (For real, this is on Harvard's undergraduate application.)
> "This final part of the application provides an opportunity for you to give us a clearer sense of you as an individual. We encourage you to write about something of direct personal importance to you. Please feel free to choose any topic. (Guideline: 250-500 words.)
> Possibilities include: your family, friends, or another person who has had an effect on you; unusual

circumstances in your life; the best or worst features in your school or community; travel or living experiences in other countries; a question we should have asked in our application; an ethical, political, or social issue that interests you or poses a challenge to you; how your college experiences (academic or nonacademic) might help you fulfill lifetime goals; how your family or the friends who know you best would describe you; which experiences or ideas or events have done the most to make you the person you are."

Daunting enough? We think so.

Nick considers what he would like to say. He has moved around with his family because his father is in the Air Force, and they have transferred many times to and from bases, but he does not want to write about his rootlessness. He wonders, what has been occupying his mind when he spaces out in American History class? Other than sex and getting out of high school, what does he think about when he daydreams? His favorite thing to do is to sit in his room and listen to music and space out. He thinks of odd music from Yemen that he listened to recently—it inspired and shocked him. Why did it do that?

STEP 2: WRITE DOWN YOUR MAIN POINT

Writing down your main point does not necessarily mean that you will use the resulting sentence in your essay, only that this sentence will exist to focus you on the point you are trying to get across. Once you have focus, every sentence in your essay will serve to sharpen that focus.

Nick writes, "When I listened to that weird Yemen music I realized that people live and grow up anywhere in the world and that seems natural to them, just like my life seems natural to me. I think it's weird to live there and they probably think it's weird to live in the U.S." He decides that writing about the way the music makes him feel, rather than the music itself, will be more helpful because he knows more about that, and it will show more about him.

STEP 3: WRITING THE ESSAY, THE ROUGH DRAFT

Once you have your main point, you know what your first paragraph will cover: an introduction of that main point. This can be done in a creative manner, and should be told as a story when possible. Most people are interested in stories. The personal essay allows you to stray from the form of the academic paper; it allows you to express yourself with vibrancy and wit and a more casual and narrative form than most other types of writing. The paragraphs following that first one amplify your main point and give clear examples. The conclusion restates the main point. Since you are writing a rough draft here, allow yourself to go over the recommended page limit if you feel like it. You can cut later; now is the time to get as much raw material on paper as you can. Experiment, gush, go on and on about your dog Charlie, or whatever strikes your fancy. You can reorganize and refine later.

STEP 4: EDIT YOUR ROUGH DRAFT

Now that you have experimented, gushed, and gotten it all down on paper, it is time to edit.

Drill One

Edit the following essay for style. You are trying to make it more concise. Delete or reconstruct any awkward sentences, and keep it lively. You may want to check back to chapter three for the questions to ask when you are editing. Make sure the essay conveys the main point that Nick outlined in his sentence. When you are finished, check the edits on the following page and look for differences.

One day this past November, when I came home from school, I was exhausted and dispirited. I thought of all the homework I had to do, and the chores I had to finish. I remembered that it was only going to get colder and rainier. I had taken some music recordings out from the library for an assignment for my music appreciation class, and I decided that this assignment would be the easiest to begin. My teacher wanted us to select music of a culture we knew nothing about and to listen to it. I had chosen music from Yemen.

I lay down on my bed and turned on the music and shut my eyes. It is not that I have never listened to music before; I listen to it as much as anyone my age, on the radio in the car, at parties, with friends. For the next fifteen minutes I listened in a way that I have not listened before.

It is difficult for me to describe the way the music sounded. It was filled with twanging curving screeches, and warbling of old men. It was not beautiful in any way I have ever considered, and I would never put it on for background music at a party. But when I listened to it I saw the world from which it came. Of course I will never really know unless I visit there whether what I imagined is really what Yemen is like. I saw sand and blue sky and children in robes. I thought of the children and I realized that there must be boys there like myself, seventeen years old and nearing the end of whatever they have for high school, and hearing this music as part of their daily life. I know western culture has permeated large sections of the world, but I thought of growing up there, or really growing up somewhere else, anywhere else. The world there is entirely different, and people exist there the same as they do here, and grow up and fight with their parents and move out and age and die. It amazed me.

I know I still have all the ethnocentrism of my culture, and I have lost a bit of the feeling that I had when listening to the music. But I remember knowing, just for a moment, how big the world is and how much there is to it, with every different person and every different country a separate specific part of the whole world.

Our Version, With Edits

Here are the edits we made. Are they similar to yours? Check for differences as well. No two people edit the same way, so don't be alarmed if you would have chosen very different rewrites. Do pay attention to the redundancies and awkward sentences that we point out, these are the types of things you will try to catch when you are editing your own writing.

already said

One day this past November, ~~when~~ I came home from school, ~~I was~~ exhausted and dispirited. I thought of all the homework I had to do, and the chores I had to finish. I remembered that (it) was only going to get colder and rainier. I had taken some music recordings out from the library for an assignment for my music appreciation class, and I decided that this assignment would be the easiest to begin. My teacher wanted us to ~~select~~ music of a culture we knew nothing about ~~and to listen to~~ it. I had chosen music from Yemen.

I lay down on my bed and turned on the music and shut my eyes. It is not that I have never listened to music before; I listen to it as much as anyone my age, on the radio in the car, at parties, with friends. For the next fifteen minutes I listened in a way that I have not listened before.

It is difficult for me to describe the way the music sounded. It was filled with twanging curving screeches, and *the* ∧ warbling of old men. It was not beautiful in any way I have ever considered, and I would never put it on for background music at a party. But when I listened to (it) I saw the world from which it came. Of course I will never really know unless I visit there whether what I imagined is really what Yemen is like. I saw sand and blue sky and children in robes. ~~I thought of the children and~~ I realized that there must be ~~boys~~ *people* there like myself, seventeen years old and

Margin notes (left):
- too many sentences begin with "I"
- need a better transition between thoughts here
- change in thought and tone—new paragraph
- why "it"?

Margin notes (right):
- what does "it" refer to?
- makes me look lazy
- listen to
- foreshado with "expecting nothing"
- unnecessa
- maybe put a "but" because t is in contrast
- *imagined I*
- they know this— ma it one wor in previou sentence
- this is a main point! put at e

nearing the end of whatever they have for high school, and

hearing this music as part of their daily life. I know western

culture has permeated large sections of the world, but I

~~thought of growing up there, or really growing up~~

~~somewhere else, anywhere else.~~ The world there is entirely

different, and people exist there the same as they do here,

and grow up and fight with their parents and move out and

age and die. It amazed me.

why tell
them this?

nonsense,
needs a
more
personal
ending

relate
back to
first ¶

   I know I still have all the ethnocentrism of my culture,

and I have lost a bit of the feeling that I had when listening

to the music. But I remember ~~knowing~~, just for a moment,

how big the world is and how much there is to it, ~~with every~~

~~different person and every different country a separate~~

~~specific part of the whole world~~.

too many
"buts"—
use
"neverthe-
less, that
music
made me
know"

STEP 5: FINAL DRAFT

Make the edits you found in step four, and polish it up. This draft
contains all the edits made in the revision process, as well as some
new edits. It has the proper paragraph format and has been checked
for spelling and other mistakes.

The version of Nick's essay we have here has some of the awkward
sentences rewritten. It is 345 words—nice and concise. See what
you think of the improvements, and how we accomplished them.
Nick can send the essay in and relax about school and go see some
soothing idiotic films.

One day this past November, I came home from school

exhausted and dispirited, thinking of all the homework to do,

and the chores to finish. November meant more cold and rain.

I dragged myself to my room to begin my homework by listening to some music for an assignment for my music appreciation class. My teacher wanted us to select music of a culture we knew nothing about, and I had chosen music from Yemen. I lay down on my bed and turned on the music and shut my eyes, expecting nothing.

I listen to music often; I listen to it on the radio in the car, at parties, with friends. But for the next fifteen minutes I listened in a way I had not listened before.

Describing the sound of the music is difficult. It was filled with twanging curving screeches, and the warbling of old men. It was not beautiful in any way I have ever considered, and I would never put it on for background music at a party. But as I listened I imagined that I saw the world from which it came. I saw sand and blue sky and children in robes. The world there is entirely different, yet people exist there the same as they do here. They grow up, fight with their parents, move out, age, and die. I was amazed. I realized that there must be boys there like myself, seventeen years old and nearing the end of whatever they have for high school, and hearing this music as part of their daily life. To them, growing up in Yemen is normal, and growing up in the United States is strange.

Hearing that music made me know, just for a moment, how big the world is and how much there is to it, of music, and cultures, and the people who make up both these things. It pulled me from the hole of my November and showed me the world, for an instant.

HOW TO WRITE IT, WITH YOUR HOSTESS HANNA

The same principles apply when you write an essay for an application to graduate school. Consider Hanna, who wants to go to business school. She will follow the same steps that Nick did. There is no real difference in the types of questions asked on college and graduate school applications, only in the experiences you will have accrued by the time you apply to graduate school, so, as always, let the truth be your guide.

STEP 1: FOCUS ON WHAT YOU WANT TO SAY

> Hanna is applying to business schools, and the following question appears in the University of California–Los Angeles application.
>
> "Please provide us with a one-page summary of personal and family background. Include information on where you grew up, parents' occupations, any siblings, and perhaps a highlight or special memory of your youth."
>
> Yes, it said a one-page summary. Of poor Hanna's whole life story, and Hanna is 25 years old. What is she to do?
>
> She considers unifying feelings she has about her childhood and family. Playing and school and siblings all mattered, but what, she considers, formed her most? Why is she going to business school anyway? That must be the focus of the application, and she wants to present herself in the most positive light possible to enhance her chances for admission. What part of her childhood most influenced her decision to attend business school? She thinks of her Aunt Susan, who visited when she was eight: Aunt Susan, on her way to law school and very excited. Hmm.

STEP 2: WRITE DOWN YOUR MAIN POINT

> Hanna writes, "When Aunt Susan visited she was happy for the first time ever and it made me happy to see her. I think she was happy because she had

direction, and now I do too." This way, she figures, she can answer the question UCLA posed, and present herself to the admissions staff as someone really serious about going to business school.

STEP 3: WRITE THE ESSAY

Hanna thinks back to that special day when her Aunt Susan visited and writes down anything and everything that she can remember. She doesn't worry about writing perfect sentences. She doesn't worry about exact chronology. She gets her thoughts down on paper—that's it.

STEP 4: EDIT YOUR ROUGH DRAFT

Edit this piece just as you edited the previous piece. Then check your edits against the version on the following page. You are trying to make the essay concise and interesting. Don't worry if your edits are not the exact same edits that appear on the following page. No two people edit the exact same way. But look for the differences, and try to analyze why the edits on the following page were chosen.

Rough Draft

I grew up in Baltimore, Maryland, with both my parents and two sisters. My father was a baker, and my mother worked as a teacher's aide. Both my parents came from large families and there were always relatives of one side or another stopping by to visit. I remember when my mother's youngest sister, my Aunt Susan, came to visit us one August.

Aunt Susan was the sister my mother always worried about, and talked to my father about over dinner. She would say Susan was unfocused, she had no steady suitor, she was wandering around doing nothing with her life even though she'd had a college education, which not all of the sibling had had. Susan was one of my favorite Aunts. She was nearest my age and the wandering that my mother worried over seemed romantic and thrilling to me.

While we waited for her my mother said, "Susan has something big to tell us. Now I don't know what it is but we should all be very supportive because any decision Susan makes has to be for the better." When Susan came we all adjourned to the kitchen table which was where all the announcements were made. Susan looked happier than I ever remember seeing her. "I've decided to go to law school," she said, "And I'm going to work for the ACLU when I get out. I'm going to help people."

I had never seen Aunt Susan sure of anything before, but it was clear she was sure now. She did go to law school, and while it was not easy along the way, she got a job with the ACLU, and works there to this day.

Seeing Aunt Susan decide she wanted something, and then watching her go an get it was thrilling. She had always been a romantic if troubled figure. With her decision and de-termination, she was not only wonderful, but also strong and happy. I think of that night often, because I feel I have come to the same point in my life, and business school is the place I will find my fulfillment.

Our Version, With Edits

I grew up in Baltimore, Maryland, with ~~both my parents~~ and two sisters. My father, was a baker, ~~and~~ my mother, ~~worked~~ as a teacher's aide. ~~Both my parents came from large families and there were always relatives of one side or another stopping by to visit.~~ I remember when my mother's youngest sister, my Aunt Susan, came to visit us one August.

make one introductory sentence

unnecessary

unnecessary, already clear

Aunt Susan was the sister my mother always worried about, discussed with and ~~talked to~~ my father ~~about~~ over dinner. She would say Susan was unfocused; ~~she had no steady suitor, she was~~ wandering around doing nothing with her life even though she'd had a college education, which not all of the siblings had had. Susan was ~~one of~~ my favorite Aunts. She was nearest my age, and the wandering that my mother worried over seemed romantic and thrilling to me.

weird wording

bad ending and need more about Aunt Susan

too wishy-washy

~~While we waited for her~~ my mother said, "Susan has something big to tell us. Now I don't know what it is but we should all be very supportive because any decision Susan makes has to be for the better." When Susan came we all adjourned to the kitchen table ~~which was~~ where all the announcements were made. Susan looked happier than I ever remember seeing her. "I've decided to go to law school," she said, "And I'm going to work for the ACLU when I get out. I'm going to help people."

unclear — say when: "the night before"

two separate thoughts

unnecessary

more dramatic starting with "she said"

I had never seen Aunt Susan sure of anything before, but it was clear she was sure now. ¶ She did go to law school, and while it was not easy along the way, she got a job with the ACLU, and works there to this day.

tense

cliché

Seeing Aunt Susan decide she wanted something, and then

typo watching her go an~~d~~ get it,was thrilling. She had always been a

(romantic if troubled) figure. With her decision and

determination, she was not only wonderful, but also strong and

happy. I think of that night often, because I feel I have come to

the same point in my life, and business school is (the place) I will — *where or how?*

find my fulfillment.

STEP 5: FINAL DRAFT

Hannah's Final Draft

I grew up in Baltimore with my father, a baker, my

mother, a teacher's aide, and my two sisters. There were always

relatives of one side or another stopping by to visit. My mother's

youngest sister, my Aunt Susan, came to visit us one August

when I was twelve.

Aunt Susan was the sister my mother always worried

about and discussed with my father over dinner. She would say

Susan was unfocused, wandering around doing nothing with her

life though she'd had a college education, something my mother

lacked. Susan was lost. Susan was in trouble. Susan was my

favorite aunt. She was nearest my age, and the wandering that

my mother worried over seemed romantic and thrilling to me.

The night before Aunt Susan was to arrive my mother

said, "Susan has something big to tell us. Now I don't know

what it is but we should all be very supportive because any decision

Susan makes has to be for the better." When Susan walked in, it was clear that something had changed. She was as fascinating as ever, with tales of her crazy, exciting life. But this time her stories revolved around a temporary job in a law office. I figured that the existence of Susan's job was her shocking announcement, big enough to account for the surprise my mother had referred to. But then Susan called us into the kitchen, where all family announcements were made. She looked happier than I had ever seen her. She said, "I've decided to go to law school, and when I'm finished I'm going to work for the ACLU. I'm going to help people."

I had never seen Aunt Susan sure of anything before, but she was clearly sure then.

Nothing in my life has made a greater impression on me than Aunt Susan's decision. While the law has never intrigued me as it did her, her desire, and her focus once she had decided what she wanted to do, thrills me still to think of it. She did go to law school, and while it was not easy along the way, she got a job with the ACLU, and works there now.

I think of that night often, because I feel I have come to a similar point in my life, and business school is my avenue to fulfillment.

WEIRD DEAD PEOPLE QUESTIONS, AND OTHER ODDITIES

When you are given less leeway in your essay question, when an application asks you to respond to a more directed question, what do you do? Some examples of recent essay questions are:

"If you could be a talk show host and you could have the opportunity to interview any three prominent persons living or deceased, whom would you choose, why, and what would you discuss?"

"Discuss an issue of personal, local, national, or international concern, and its importance to you."

"Select a creative work: a novel, film, poem, musical piece, painting, or other work of art that has influenced the way you view the world and the way you view yourself. Discuss the work and its effect on you."

"Highlight your academic accomplishments."

"Tell us how a form of art or entertainment has affected you."

These essays follow the rules of all nonfiction writing—be honest and write about a subject that has meaning for you.

As for the dead people, there is that fine line between cliché and greatness. Don't go after the big names—Einstein, Lincoln, Washington—without a very good reason for wanting to talk with them. Often a writer will invoke these names in the blind hope that some of their greatness will rub off on the writer. Not so. The schools that request these types of essays are not doing so because they want to see if you can identify what a great person is, they are doing it because they want to know more about you personally, and your individual way of seeing the world. If, however, you are truly obsessed with some other great personage, by all means use him or her. Try to select people you would truly like to speak with, and your personality will shine through.

Basically, the other essay questions here ask you to present one particular facet of yourself, so you must focus on only one in your essay. If you are asked about your most important experience, describe one that illuminates your strengths. No one else is going to go around saying how great you are, except your recommenders of course, and no matter how well your recommenders know you, you know yourself better. Qualities worth highlighting on a college or graduate school application: diligence, responsibility, honesty, tenacity, resilience in the face of difficulty, creativity (particularly in the case of finding solutions for problems), curiosity (both academic and otherwise). And as you will read again and again: be honest. Every human being in the world has some good qualities, and the only way to write this sort of essay well and cogently is to tell the truth. If you cannot identify any characteristics you think impress a school, ask friends and other loved ones. They have that perfect blend of objectivity and affection, and you will probably walk around grinning like an idiot after you get your list of qualities. (You might want to consider doing this even if you already know what you want to put in your essay.) You may feel embarrassed writing about yourself in such a self-aggrandizing manner; just keep in mind that you were asked to do so.

LET'S TALK ABOUT US FOR A WHILE

"How will University X help further your career goals?"

"Discuss your reasons for wanting to attend Y University; how does it differ from other schools on your list?"

When a school asks you to talk about the school, don't think they just want pure flattery. Of course, they want to hear positive things, but the hitch is they want to hear *informed*, positive things. The key here is to do a bit of research. Ask your guidance counselor what departments are particularly noted at the particular university. Read the materials and find out what the university considers its best features; is it small with a terrific student-to-teacher ratio or is it large with fabulous research facilities? Use guides and identify what students consider the university's strengths and weaknesses. Then, consider what you want. Figure where the university's strengths intersect with your desires and write about that. You don't need to mention what you consider its drawbacks.

COMMON PERSONAL ESSAY PITFALLS

DAY BY DAY BY DAY BY DAY BY...
Don't feel tied to chronology. You are asked to produce a personal essay because the asker wants to know something further about *you*.

This does not necessarily mean that your essay must a include detailed biography. You can indicate more about yourself by discussing your thoughts on current events or morality or scientific ethics. You can tell a story about your life, but it does not necessarily have to be set as a straight biography beginning with the day you were born and detailing each event to the present. Stick to what really interests you and you'll have a more interesting essay.

HAVING NO POINT

A personal essay is not a mandate to list the events of your life. Before you start writing, have an idea of what you intend to say. You must have a main point. Your main point can be that you learned through many years of shopping for shoes that shopping was for you an opportunity to understand capitalism and our culture. Your main point can be that by watching the film *Bambi* you realized how transitory and powerful the idea of life on this earth is for you. Whatever you write about, you must have a point in mind. Simply listing the events in your life will lead you to write a journal entry, not an essay.

BEING KoOky

Most people fear that they are boring, and that the admissions officer for whatever program they are applying to will certainly realize this and look at their essays and say, "Well, I've seen a million essays about working in a laboratory over the summer," or taking piano lessons, or being a camp counselor, etc. To make themselves stand apart, these folks think of the oddest KRAZIEST thing they do and write about that. Before you run out and write your essay about your encounter with space aliens, remember our guideposts: Clarity and Honesty. If you don't really believe that eating fried fire ants in the desert was important for you, for goodness sake, don't write about it. Not only will you misrepresent yourself, but you will also be writing about something you don't really care about, which leads to muddled, messy work. Your perspective makes an essay interesting, not the actual subject. While many phenomena are common, people are singular, and your particular experience and the angle from which you saw it can be duplicated by no one else on this earth. Therefore, that view, that particular perspective, is what you should aim to convey in your essay.

GETTING TOO DETAILED

When you write a personal essay you may get into territory most readers are not too familiar with: your family, your town, etc. While it is necessary to introduce characters or settings with which your reader may be unfamiliar, "My friend Toby," or "The dump down the hill from my house," it is unhelpful to describe anything in greater detail than the essay really calls for. It is probably unnecessary to inform the reader of Toby's hair color unless you are writing an essay regarding a major hair-dyeing trauma you experienced.

BEING OVERLY DRAMATIC

"The day I dyed my hair so I would look more like Toby was the most momentous day of my life." Think for a moment, is this really true? Or are you trying to get your reader interested by yelling, in effect, "Over here, over here! Big things!" When you reread your essay, be sure to check for words such as "ever," "never," and "the most." Allow your thoughts and ideas to be the drama of the moment. Remember, the reader is already reading the essay. By getting overly dramatic you make your writing seem desperate to be noticed, which is no more attractive in prose than it is in people.

AVOID REDUNDANCY

People are tempted to begin sentences with, "I think," or "I believe." In a personal essay, this is bad form. If you are writing the essay, then anything you write is something you think, feel, or believe. To say so explicitly is redundant.

AVOID EXCESSIVE INFORMALITY

Just because you are writing about something personal is no reason for your prose to become casual or intimate. While you have room for a certain relaxation in a personal essay, do not let your writing become a mere record of a conversation. Your aim is clarity, so excessive folksiness is to be avoided. Your ideas will allow the reader to view you as you are, and the way to present them clearly is to write them clearly.

SWEETHEART, DON'T HIDE YOUR LIGHT UNDER A BUSHEL

As frightened or embarrassed or insecure as you may feel responding to one of the "Why are *you* so great?" statements, these ask you to present yourself as well as you can, so don't be afraid to boast. The reader will not think you are being conceited, she will realize you are fulfilling the assigned task.

WORRYING ABOUT LENGTH

The only length consideration that should occupy you is staying within the guidelines given. Do not exceed the suggested length of an essay. And what of essays that are too short, you ask? There is no such thing. Figure out what you want to say and then say it well. However much space that takes up is as long as your essay should be.

LAZINESS

Don't write one essay listing reasons you want to go to a particular college or university and then repeat it for each school, changing the name. They can tell and it won't be your best effort.

HONESTY TO A FAULT

Don't write that the reason you want to go to a particular school is that you consider it a safety school.

SPECIFICS

There is no set format for references in a personal essay. Many writers include mentions of their favorite authors, books, or other things that may have influenced them on their subject, but such references are listed in the essay and not given as part of any sort of bibliography.

Personal essays should be double spaced for easier reading. However, if you are asked to keep your remarks to the length of one page, you can write in a single-spaced format.

Indent your paragraphs; don't use an extra space.

Titles are unnecessary in the personal essay; unless you can think of a really great one, don't use a title.

AND THUS...

Personal application essays ask you to present your personal side. You must be honest and forthcoming, writing about something that matters to you. As long as you present a true passion of yours and you check your work for the pitfalls described above, you can be sure your essay will have the impact and the originality required.

Book List

These books contain personal essays on a wide variety of subjects, and reading them will give you great ideas on how creative and satisfying a personal essay can be.

Roger Kahn, *The Boys Of Summer*, HarperCollins.

Rick Bass, *Winter* and *Oil Notes*, Houghton Mifflin.

Jim Harrison, *Just Before Dark*, Houghton Mifflin/Seymour Lawrence.

Phillip Lopate, editor: *The Art of The Personal Essay: An Anthology from the Classical Era to the Present*, Anchor Books.

Anna Quindlen, *Thinking Out Loud*, Random House.

William Strunk and E. B. White, *The Elements of Style*, Macmillan.

CHAPTER 6

Reviews, Articles, and Essay Tests

C ertainly when given time to research, outline, and edit, one
can write a serviceable term paper, but in an exam situation,
how does one write an essay?

Q: Please compare and contrast how you write an essay for an
essay question test with how you write a research paper, giving
examples where appropriate.

A: The same way you write an essay in any other situation, but
faster.

THE
LEARNER'S PERMIT WRITTEN TEST :
Essay Questions

1 In the style of Edna Ferber, contrast and
compare thruway, freeway, highway, and turnpike.

2. Two authors approach an intersection at the same moment. One has
eleven books under his belt (all of which did o.k.). The other has only
one, but it was a massive *best seller* as well as a <u>critical</u> <u>success</u>.
Who has the right of way? Why?

3 A bus, a taxi, a stretch limousine, a Dodge Dart, and a Mercedes plow
into each other on Broadway and 97th Street at rush hour. Write about the incident
from the viewpoints of the drivers of each vehicle in each of their respective dialects.

4 Write a sonnet about parallel parking

5 Choose three of the following signs and explain their metaphysical
meanings in all of post-Freudian literature.

You can use the following format for all types of non-personal
essays, such as editorials, reviews, and creative nonfiction. You should
also look to the end of the chapter for recommended reading on
these types of essays. Reading great versions of a literary form can
inspire you to write great versions.

FORMAT

INTRODUCTION

An introduction is a one-sentence response to the question. Essentially, how you would respond if you weren't forced to write an entire page on the subject.

BODY OF THE ESSAY

The body of the essay includes in most cases three (sometimes more or fewer) paragraphs, with specific examples in support of the answer you present in your introduction.

CONCLUSION

The conclusion is a restatement of your introduction, with some notes on how the intervening examples clearly support your contention.

HOW TO WRITE IT, WITH YOUR HOSTESS ROSE

STEP 1: RESEARCH

The research for your essay must take place before you go in to take your test. It's called studying, remember? You will likely have a basic idea of what the test will be about, so you must read the background material, your textbook, and any additional assigned readings as though you had to write a paper about the subject. You want to know what you are talking about so you can form opinions (your introduction and conclusion) and support them with clear evidence (the supporting paragraphs and examples that make up the body of your paper). These are the essential aims of studying anyway.

> Rose's upcoming test on the history of basketball will definitely include an essay question. The test is to be about the 1992-93 basketball season, and will focus primarily on the Eastern Conference teams. Rose goes to the library and studies the sports pages on microfilm, periodicals of the time, and her textbook. She hopes for a question on Patrick Ewing and his greatness; she dreads a question on Dominique Wilkins. She struggles, she hopes, she dreams, but most of all, she prepares.

STEP 2: TAKE THE TEST

Generally an essay test will have more than two essay questions. You should try to do these questions in the order in which you find them on the test, the first question first, the second second, and so on. But, if you find yourself looking at the first essay question and not knowing how to answer it, do not waste time attempting to bullshit your way through. If you have extra time at the end of the test you can go back, but it is best to focus your time on the questions you know how to answer.

STEP 3: OUTLINE

These questions deserve very brief outlines. The outlines need not even be written down; nevertheless, they must be thought through. Do not make life needlessly difficult for yourself by writing without knowing what you are writing. Figure out your topic sentence, then your three examples; then you can begin.

Rose goes in to class on the day of the test. She has extra pens in case one runs out of ink. She has gotten sufficient sleep the previous three nights. She is ready for anything. The test begins with true-or-false questions; she breezes through these. Then, the essay: "Compare and contrast Patrick Ewing and Shaquille O'Neal as they performed over the course of the 1992-93 basketball season, and decide which of the two you think should have been the starting center of the All-Star game."

She quickly writes:

Ewing was the better center. (1) better leadership of team (2) more control over whole game, not just his performance, and (3) not a show-off.

Her outline is now complete; she is ready to start writing.

STEP 4: WRITING

Essays written under timed conditions leave less room for posturing. The pressure of time forces you to think of what you want to say,

say it, and proceed. This can lead to better writing in general, because you are forced to say what you mean. Do not be intimidated by those who sit at desks near yours and ask the teacher for additional blue books or paper. Length is not in and of itself a virtue. The more succinctly you express yourself, the better your essay will be, so do not spend time thinking about the fanciest way to write something, just write it.

In the paragraphs that make up the body of the essay (the exception being the one-paragraph essay in which you simply state the examples that support your conclusion), you must clearly present the supporting evidence, and then show how that evidence supports your point. It is not enough to say that there were high taxes on tea at the time and people in Boston were unhappy. You must also note that this demonstrates that there was ample reason for revolution.

Rose Begins Her Essay

INTRO

Two of the most important centers in the Eastern conference over the 1992-93 season were Patrick Ewing of the New York Knickerbockers, and Shaquille O'Neal of the Orlando Magic. Both are magnificent athletes, and they have similarities as well as differences, but in any comparison, Patrick Ewing is a better center and deserved to start in the All-Star game.

COMPARE AND CONTRAST

The two players were very similar. Both were high-scoring centers, both excelled in the college game, and both were the number-one draft picks of their respective years. Yet it is important to note that these years were very different. O'Neal came out of the draft in 1992, so the 92-93 season was his first. Ewing was drafted in 1985. During the 1992-93 season Ewing was just reaching the height of his considerable powers. His experience and maturity would lend an important resonance to the Eastern All-Star team.

EWING BETTER

They both played the role of the outstanding player of their particular teams. But this role, and the ways they performed in it, also demonstrates some of their differences, and shows why, and how, Ewing was the more appropriate choice for All-Star center.

REASON 1

As the star of his team, Ewing did an outstanding job in scoring, rebounds, and assists. Thus, he not only played well for himself, making himself a better player, but he made his team a better team. One of the most important developments of the 92-93 season was the offensive presence of John Starks. Clearly, Starks could not have come to the fore unless Ewing had played in such a way as to help develop another outstanding player.

While some may say that Ewing was surrounded by better players, this is not enough to prove that the centers' differences resulted solely from their teams. Most glaring among O'Neal's weaknesses of that season was his self-congratulatory play. A smashed backboard may have looked impressive at the time, but it was only another piece of evidence showing that O'Neal wanted his *playing* to be noticed. Contrast that with Ewing, who never asked for attention, but worked his absolute hardest so that his team would be noticed, and win.   **REASON 2**

The many reasons mentioned here: experience in the National Basketball Association, leadership ability, and generous play, provide sufficient evidence that during the 1992-93 season, Patrick Ewing was a better center, and a better player, than Shaquille O'Neal, and thus would have been the best choice for the starting center for the Eastern All-Star team.   **CONCLUSION**

STEP 5: DOES YOUR ESSAY ANSWER THE QUESTION?

This is *very important*. Sometimes you may go off on a tangent that interests you, and in doing so provide a strong base for your response to the question without actually answering it. If so, simply add a paragraph that more fully responds to what you have been asked.

STEP 6: PROOFREADING

While proofreading is always a part of writing, it takes a slightly different form in a test situation. You do not have much time, so you must restrict your check to flagrant errors of meaning and form. A sentence that expresses what you mean in a slightly awkward form does not have to be rewritten in a testing environment. If your teacher had intended you to create a perfectly written piece, he would have assigned theses topics as essays to take home rather than to be written under timed conditions in class. Your essay must (1) make sense, and (2) answer the question asked. These are your two main criteria when proofing.

STEP 7: HAND THAT BABY IN

And pat yourself on the back, too—you did it.

COMMON PITFALLS

BULLSHIT

There are those of us who, even if caught red-handed with the Mona Lisa outside the Louvre Museum in Paris, would be able to talk our way out of the situation—in French. If this description does not include you, do not attempt to talk your way out of not knowing the answer to an essay question. Your teacher has seen it all before, and will be neither convinced nor impressed.

BAD HANDWRITING

Remember all that "neatness counts" stuff from second grade? Well, remember that the person who wrote this test for you has to grade it as well, and if she cannot read what you wrote, then no matter how brilliant your essay is, you will not get a good grade on it. Try to be aware of this as you write. Slow down, and use print letters instead of cursive; that may help.

THE KITCHEN SINK

An essay usually calls for three examples. In some circumstances you may be called upon to present as many as five. Include more than five examples and you are suffering from the dreaded verbal diarrhea. Remember that whoever created this test also has to read it. She wants to know that you understand the subject and can back up your understanding with documentation. Going beyond this becomes tedious and kills trees.

SPECIFICS

Essays on examinations require no particular format other than the paragraph form. Be sure to indent and use full sentences.

When using references in an essay test, the first time, write the title of the book or article and the author, unless it is a textbook, which needs no reference. When referring to a book or article after you have already written out the title, use the last name of the author.

AND THUS. . .

Teachers ask you to write an essay on an examination to test your knowledge of the subject (as in, did you study?) and your ability to convey that knowledge in a succinct and logical manner. Oblige them.

BOOK LIST

These books contain essays of a less personal nature than most. Any would be helpful to read for inspiration when writing a personal essay, or writing any sort of non-personal essay, such as a review, editorial, or creative nonfiction.

Mike Davis, *City of Quartz*, London Press.

M. F. K. Fisher, *The Art of Eating*, Collier Books.

Fran Lebowitz, *Social Studies*, Pocket Books, and *Metropolitan Life*, E.P. Dutton.

John McPhee, *The John McPhee Reader*, Farrar, Straus and Giroux.

Flannery O'Connor, *Mystery and Manners*, Noonday Press.

George Plimpton, *Hank Aaron: One For The Record*, Bantam Books.

William Strunk and E. B. White, *The Elements of Style*, Macmillan.

Any of the *Best American Essays* series, published by Ticknor Fields.

CHAPTER 7

Research
Papers

For many people, the research paper is the most daunting academic task. You can rest assured, however, that it is by no means impossible. Once you have a clear plan of attack, writing the research paper, though arduous, is no more difficult than following an intricate recipe for chocolate cake.

FORMAT

A research paper is nothing more than a glorified long essay, so it will have the same basic construction.

INTRODUCTION

Some papers will ask you to prove some sort of argument and others will ask only for loads of information about a subject. If you are trying to prove a thesis, indicate that during the introduction. If you are writing a purely informative paper, set forth the subject of the paper in the introduction along with the aspects of the subject you intend to discuss.

BODY OF THE PAPER
The body of the paper consists of the information you have garnered through your extensive research. In a paper that presents an argument, the body includes a cogent support of the argument. It also includes one section for the opposition's case, which you then endeavor to disprove. You make your own argument much more convincing by allowing the reader to see the counter-arguments made, and then a reasoned rebuttal of such.

In an informational paper, the body presents all the research on your subject, in a logical and organized manner.

Separate your research into themes, and then build the paper theme by theme, using paragraphs to separate your themes. In a paper of over twenty-five pages paragraphing may not be sufficient to separate your themes. In that case, subsections may be necessary, and within subsections, paragraphing. Whatever format you select, make sure you maintain it consistently throughout your paper.

Research papers also allow for other media such as photographs and illustrations, so the body of the paper often includes both text and visual material. Take full advantage of this and use them where appropriate to accent and allow the reader to attach visual images to the text. A research paper is like a long magazine article, and what usually interests you in long magazine articles? Not just the information presented but also the manner in which it is displayed and—let's be honest here—the fancy pictures. A research paper should be interesting, and pleasing layout can be an important part of that.

The body of the paper refers to sources quite regularly, as that is the aim of a research paper. Any direct quotes from sources or paraphrases from research sources are footnoted. This means, after a quote or paraphrase, put a number (these references will go in order of the paper) and at the bottom of the page (the foot, get it?) you write the source of the note, including title, author, publisher. You will find more information on how to write footnotes in the Specifics section of this chapter.

CONCLUSION
The conclusion restates the main point and indicates how the paper has accomplished it. If your paper argued for a particular thesis, reiterate how that thesis was proved by the successive examples. If your paper described a phenomenon, summarize the information presented and what it showed you.

BIBLIOGRAPHY
Here you will indicate the sources you used for the information you presented in the paper. Anything you read that aided you in your understanding of the subject is included here according to the guidelines described in the Specifics section of this chapter.

HOW TO WRITE A RESEARCH PAPER, WITH TIM

STEP 1: THE TOPIC
Some teachers may assign a specific topic, but most will provide a possible range and allow you to select your own. A research paper is an opportunity for your teacher or professor to assess your research and writing skills. Typically, your instructor will assign a paper of some generally specified length—5, 10, or 20 pages—on some broad range of topics. "Cover some important issue about Colonial history in the early 1800s," she might say. It is then up to you to select the exact topic, find out all there is to know about it, and write the thing. For instance, our friend Tim might be assigned a paper.

> Tim is taking a class in Nutritional Sociology and his teacher announces, "A five-page research paper on some way sugar's influence is seen in our society, due in one month. I expect you to research and annotate this responsibly."

The most important criteria for a topic are its interest to you and the breadth of the topic.

INTEREST TO YOU

If the topic you select holds no appeal, it is very doubtful your paper will be interesting to you or your reader. This can lead to problems, because if you are not interested, it will be that much more difficult to get yourself to write the darn thing, and what you do write will not be your best. Even if the range of topics does not light your fire, try to find an angle that does. You may not be interested in the Reconstruction Era South in general, but you may be interested in the race relations, health care, or leisure activities of that time. A bit of research here into the general range from which you have to choose can be extremely beneficial. Read for things that catch your interest. Look at titles of books for ideas on what other writers have been interested in; you may be inspired.

Tim reads up on sugar at the library. He talks to people in the street about sugar. He eats a packet of sugar straight out of the sugar bowl in a restaurant, provoking complaints to the management from other customers. He listens to "A spoonful of sugar makes the medicine go down" and briefly considers writing his paper about sugar in the modern American musical; his research is blocked by his inability to find any other references to sugar in musicals, with the notable exception of *Charlie and the Chocolate Factory*, which he finds frighteningly hallucinatory. He is seen walking through the street clutching a bag of sugar and shaking his head, bewildered.

BREADTH OF TOPIC

This is generally the stickiest issue for writers of papers. You want your topic to be small enough to cover in a paper, but broad enough that you can wring 10 or 20 pages out of it. Though you would be astounded on what people can base a 200-page book, a paper on the Reconstruction Era South would probably need closer to 1,000 pages, while the sash of Robert E. Lee's uniform would probably fill only one good paragraph.

> Tim briefly considers a paper about sugar in general, then goes to the library and finds 250 books on that topic. Too many. He regroups and considers a paper about the first bite of a candy bar; is it different from the other bites? He returns to the library, finds nothing. He plunges into blackest depression.

STEP 2: CHECK TOPIC WITH THE PROFESSOR OR TEACHER

Before you begin slogging through obscure tomes searching for the perfect quote, make sure the topic you have chosen is an acceptable one. There is very little worse than starting a huge bulk of research or writing only to find out that it was all for nothing. If your topic is off the mark, your teacher can guide you to one more suitable. You can't lose by asking.

> Tormented, Tim visits his teacher after class. He confesses his troubles and she says, "The first bite of a candy bar?"
>
> "Yes," sobs Tim. "It's the part of a candy bar I love best."
>
> "Well," she says, "if it's candy bars you're interested in, why don't you do some work on that? Myself I'm a Milky Way fan. I love nougat."
>
> Tim nods to himself and thinks, "She's just the type to like a Milky Way. Sweet, but a trifle dull." Then he considers this: could it be that specific personality types like specific candy bar types? Thrilled, he proposes this thesis to his teacher, carefully avoiding any mention of Milk Way lovers as unexciting. Intrigued, she approves his paper topic.

STEP 3: NOTES & RESEARCH

Your main task is to find out as much as you can about your topic. You may be writing a research paper in which you are arguing for one thesis or another, or you may be describing a particular situation or phenomenon. Go to the library and find as many books about your topic as you can. Investigate periodicals, too. You can look in the *Readers' Guide to Periodical Literature*, usually kept up at the reference desk near the librarian. Look in the subject guides and see what articles have been published about your subject in the last year or two. If you see any that look applicable, find them. Ask your librarian for help; librarians are terrific and very willing to assist anyone in this type of situation. Maybe you'll get lucky and your article will be on microfilm and you will get to use the cool microfilm machine. Also ask your librarian about using the library computer to help with your research. Even if you're not comfortable with computers, the librarian will be able to show you how to use one without fear.

It is not necessary for you to read every word of every book or article you find. Once you have amassed a collection, look through the tables of contents of the books and read those chapters that seem applicable. Look in the bibliography of these books for suggestions of other books that might be helpful.

As you collect your reference material you should start taking notes. The jury is out as to whether index cards or legal pads are more helpful. The truth is, whichever method makes you feel more organized and businesslike is the one to use. It is imperative that your notes be taken in an organized manner, because often this stage of the paper allows you to get your thinking done, and the more organized and clear your thinking, the better your paper. For each book or article you read you should have a separate set of cards. At the top of each card put the title of the book from which the notes were gathered. Then, at the top right corner of the card mark how this note applies to your paper. This can be even easier if you use color coding. For instance, if your paper describes the sexual life of presidents, you might put the title of the book on the left, *The Best and the Brightest,* and on the right a red mark indicating that this book is about Kennedy. Keep a master list explaining all your color codes and other reference marks in case you confuse yourself. Writing down quotes from books that strike you as important or particularly relevant is also helpful. Noting the page number here will come in handy when you want to footnote. Set aside a list of illustrations and photographs related to your subject.

Tim spends the next two weeks at the library, poring over psychiatric journals and candy wrappers. He sets up a complex cross-coding system involving colors and shapes. Cards related to daring types he marks with a triangle, stay-at-homes he marks with a square, tormented souls get a circle. Caramel candy bars are yellow, mint is green, mixtures are purple.

Nougat Quarterly   ◯

According to Professor Whipt, those who like nougat are
often confused as to what nougat actually consists of, and
what the difference is between caramel and nougat. Many
teens admitted to eating nougat before listening to heavy
metal music and joining satanic cults. Connection???
"Nougat seemed to be the only substance to offer the
subjects comfort." p. 73, article titled "An important study"

Tim has been working feverishly at the library. So thrilled is he by Professor Whipt's article that he looked in the *Readers' Guide to Periodical Literature* listing by author and found three more articles by Whipt written in the past year. Tim collects fifty cards; his confidence grows. He knows he has something here.

STEP 4: MAKE AN OUTLINE

Once you have most of your research completed you are ready to begin your outline.

An outline is absolutely indispensable for a research paper because it gives you an idea of what you are writing and what you need to write next. Also, since it separates your paper into discreet chunks (an unpleasant image, no?), if you get sick to death of writing a particular section, you can just start writing another section that appears more interesting.

An outline is a sort of annotated table of contents for your research paper, and writing this outline provides you with an opportunity to organize your thoughts and your paper. The outline then provides you with a structure.

WRITE YOUR STATEMENT OF PURPOSE

You already have an idea of the subject of your paper, now you need to describe this subject with some sort of concise statement. For example: The purpose of this paper is to compare the courting rituals of men and women in late-twentieth-century urban areas.

ORGANIZE YOUR CARDS

Separate your cards into the order in which you want to refer to their topics. Depending on the length of your paper, you may have 3 to 30 subcategories. Try to organize them so that related subjects are close together, and there is some sort of natural transition between paragraphs.

WRITE YOUR CONCLUSION

We know, you've already written your statement of purpose in the first part of the outline, but it can only help to make it clearer to yourself, and the conclusion should refer to the organizational structure you've set up to support it.

Tim considers, at home with his note cards. Just what is his thesis? What does his research lead him to? He knows there is a psychology to which chocolate bars different people choose, but what is it? He writes:

Thesis: Candy bars and personality, is there a connection? Yes.

Tim consults his note cards and orders them into a logical thought process.

I. Psychology has long posited that there is a strong connection between the types of foods we eat and our psyches.
    A. Hogg's study of food and society.
       1. Quote about judging society by food on card 2.
       2. How long study went on.
    B. Weird nutritional shakes in American society.
       1. Calvinist.
    C. Food preferences of people throughout history
       1. Pres. Clinton
       2. Romans

III. Snickers, other mixed versions
    A. People desperate for action
IV. Caramels
    A. Sentimentality
       1. quote on card 7.
V. Nut bars
    A. The tough guy: peanuts and machismo
VI. Solid chocolate bar
    A. high-minded? or
    B. repressed?
VII. Coconut bars
    A. sometimes you feel like a nut?
       1. Psychopaths and coconut.
VIII. Butterfingers, toffee bars, Heath
    A. are they really classier than the rest of us?
IX. The opposition, the idea of taste as personal issue
    A. Card 24, Dr. Faust says there is no connection, we all have free will.
    B. Card 26, Dr. Pheelgud says taste changes over eras
X. Rebuttal
    A. Swiss studies, television commercials
    B. Fashion analogy
XI. Conclusion. The connection between candy bars and personality cannot be ignored, and allows us all to know more about sugar and the world we live in, and the way it affects us.

Tim sets his paper down next to the ordered cards, sets his books next to them, and takes a well-deserved break.

STEP 5: CHECK YOUR PLAN

When your outline is finished you should have a paragraph-by-paragraph plan of attack. Do you know what each paragraph is to be about? Does each paragraph support your statement of purpose? If the topic of the paper is in the form of a question, does your outline answer it? When you can answer yes to these questions, you are officially ready to write.

STEP 6: WRITE A ROUGH DRAFT

Many writers prefer to leave the writing of their introductory paragraph till the end, when they know exactly what they will be introducing. You probably want to start writing the paragraph that will follow the introduction, the paragraph in which you begin discussion of the topic. Here, your research index cards will come in handy. You already have your cards organized for each paragraph; now use them, making clear your quotes and paraphrases with footnotes, and presenting the findings of all that research. Follow your outline carefully, going paragraph by paragraph, keeping your cards in order for easy reference by the end. Give yourself plenty of time; burnout and exhaustion lead to sloppy writing. When you get to the end you can write your introductory and conclusive paragraphs, which will be fairly similar.

STEP 7: TAKE A DAY OFF, THEN REREAD & EDIT THE PAPER

Once you have written your paper according to the form of your outline, you have what is known as the first draft. You will probably want to take a day off after finishing the first draft to give yourself some breathing room before you come back to edit it. Make sure one paragraph flows smoothly to the next. Make sure you have given credit where credit is due. When paraphrasing or quoting you MUST credit the source, inserting footnotes as you go along.

QUESTIONS TO ASK WHEN YOU ARE EDITING YOUR PAPER

- Do I make a convincing case for my point?

- Do I present the story of whatever I'm describing in an interesting and engaging manner?

- Are both my arguments and the opposition's arguments clearly presented?

- Does each paragraph serve a clear function either in describing the phenomenon or arguing the case?

- Do the sentences flow logically?

- Does each sentence serve a clear function in its paragraph?

If you find an unnecessary paragraph or sentence, eliminate it. If you have not made your point, look to find where you have strayed from your outline. Rewrite any illogical sentences. If you have a trusted friend you may want to have her read it, but bear in mind you will then be eternally in her debt. This is all a lot of work but it is work that is absolutely essential for a good paper. Also check for misspellings and grammatical mistakes. Make sure you read your paper through at least twice, correcting errors as you go along. Once you have edited and cleaned up any errors, you are ready for the final touches.

Editing Drill for the Research Paper

Edit Tim's five-page paper, paying attention to the editing guidelines in chapter four. We mean it; we actually want you to write in the book. Get a red pen and go. Then compare with the edits in the section following this paper.

Candy Bars and Psychology

Psychology has long posited a connection between the psyche and taste in food. The noted professor of food and psychology, Ima Hogg, says, "While many attempt to discover the secrets of the mind through outmoded techniques of psychoanalysis and clinical psychology, the true frontier on which we are discovering the key to personality is by assessing what people eat. Beyond this we cannot hope to go further." (WRITE IN FOOTNOTE FOR HOGG'S STUDY) Hogg's studies relating diet and psychosis went on for over twenty-five years, and they clearly show what any reasonable person has long suspected: you are what you eat. Think of the current fad of liquid diet shakes, so appropriate to our American society, caught between the Calvinist puritanism of our history and the relentless greed and self-indulgence of our current market economy. Consider President Clinton and his fondness for fast food, the food of a person of action, someone ready to lead! Or remember the self-destructive habits of the romans, fulfilling the slightest desire with loads of tempting delicacies, then running off to the vomitoria to rid themselves and begin again. This demonstrates a clear connection between what one eats and who one is. And indeed, the existence of a connection between food and personality points to the likelihood of a connection between candy bar choice and personality disorder.

Many studies have been done to test this theory and the results of them are here.

Much has been written about those candy bars that combine the various candy elements: nougat, caramel, nuts. The desire for all the things at once, the inability to make any sort of a concrete choice is typical of the boy/man who suffers from the peter pan syndrome, and the combination bar is his candy of choice. This is evidenced on grounds both academic and emotional. In her ground-breaking treatise on the subject, Dr. Lotta Kaloreese interviewed a group of 2,500 male participants between the ages of 23 and 55. Of those who said they were either involved or willing to be involved in what they themselves termed a mature lifestyle, only 19.7% indicated the combination bar, or "Snickers," as their primary candy choice. Of those who professed a longing to return to childhood, or to remain a child indefinitely, an astonishing 78% indicated a strong preference for the Snickers bar as their primary candy choice. (CITE KALOREESE'S STUDY) Numerical results this overwhelming cannot be ignored: Snickers is the bar of those who would be children forever.

Another stunning example is the historical references of the caramel. One of the most traditional forms of confection, the caramel is the choice of those who are overly sentimental and prone to emotional outbursts and flights of fancy. Many soft-hearted artists have long called the caramel their favorite, with laudatory remarks often taking the form of song and poetry. "Boy, there's nothing a like better than a chocolate bar with caramel in it." (CHECK MLA, DO I NEED TO FOOTNOTE THIS IF I HAVE HIS NAME?) says Barry Manilow, renowned emotional person. This sort of confession is seen over and over again in memoirs of emotional people. In writings by John Denver, Sally Field, Tchaikovsky, and other softies one can find multiple references to caramel. This happens too frequently to be mere happenstance, one has yet another reason to believe that there must be some connection between the form of candy sugar takes, and the type of person who wants that candy.

Yet another example is apparent in the strong connection between nut bars and those who love them, the tough guys both male and female. While much has been written on the connection between nuts of all types and risk-taking daredevils, including the tie between skydiving and various types of nut brittle, the clearest delineation of candy to personality is peanuts to machismo. The study was done is most particularly seen in the desire of river guides, hunters, and rock climbers for Mr. Goodbar, the peanut chocolate bar. (RICH) Dr. Rich performed his study over two years in all the venues mentioned. He used three groups among each participants. To the first group he offered a buffet table at the end of their trips which contained fruit, chocolate bars of assorted types other than Mr. Goodbars, arranged with the Mr. Goodbars at the back less reachable part of the table, with the fruit and other candy toward the front. The participants— 94% of them—reached to the back to get their Mr. Goodbars.

Several, 62% of those who chose the Mr. Goodbar, were heard to grunt the word "Good." Upon taking the bar. Dr. Rich considered the possibility that these participants had chosen the bars because they were at the back and therefore more difficult to reach and therefore a greater "prize" to these rough and tumble participants, and to try to weed these out he set up another buffet at which the Mr. Goodbars were set near the front in easy reach, no challenge at all. Again an overwhelming majority, 86% this time, chose the Mr. Goodbar over any other candy. His final group was served with a mixed buffet on which the candy was arranged every which way, with the results the same. This buffet was, in fact, picked clean of all peanut related candy, with fruit and other candy left strewn apart, due, he hypothesizes, to the desire of "macho" individuals for a hunt for their prey. On returning to his University to organize and publish his findings he tried a control group, and offered an audience of 2,000 anthropology students the same buffet. Only an astonishing 21% chose the Mr. Goodbar, and the candy proportions were the same. There can be no clearer evidence than this that there is indeed, a correlation between candy type and personality.

Scientific reason would lead one to consider whether this applied to only the nut bar, or the caramel. Recent research in the chocolate bar field has uncovered some startling findings. People who purchase the plain chocolate and milk chocolate bars generally complain of a feeling of a life left unfulfilled, of feelings and possibilities left unexplored. (WHOEVER) Similar studies of randomly selected buyers of toffee bars, including the Heath and the Skor bar indicate that these buyers, or at least 89% of these buyers, can be classified as suffering from superiority complexes, defined as the strong belief that they are better than the rest of us. The compelling evidence linking the lover of coconut bars and the psychopath only cements the bond.

There are many in both the scientific and confectionery community who protest that chocolate bar preference is merely a matter of personal taste, and hence unrelated to any personality quirks. Most notable among these groups are Dr. Faust and Dr. Pheelgud. Dr. Faust notes that much as the experiments have done to set up control groups, the studies done have not covered a wide enough expanse of the population. FOOTNOTE? OR LATER ON? In fact, all the studies, he notes, have been done in the United States where the candy bars advertise their images via television commercials. Thus it is these media images of the bars that people respond to, not the bars themselves. Dr. Pheelgud notes in his book, Candy Bars and Personality: There's No Connection, that candy bars and what goes in them changes over time, for instance licorice is not nearly as popular as it was in the early forties. PHEELGUD This change over time indicates to her that there is no real correlation, because that would indicate a change in human personality type within the space of a decade, and this she considers unlikely.

While these doctors are to be commended for their dogged attempts to discover the truth, their arguments cannot withstand scientific scrutiny. Dr. Faust is correct in noting that the studies have been done for the most part in the United States, but he ignores the important Swiss chocolate series of the Kiss Institute and the Mousse inquiries of the Academe Francais. AF As for his contention that television affects the subjects ability to respond in an unbiased manner toward the candy bar, he forgets that the images subjects respond to are not those projected by the candy company. For instance, as discussed earlier, Mr. Goodbar is loved by those who attempt to prove their prowess in sports and outdoor pursuits, yet the advertised image of Mr. Goodbar is as a friendly "fun" sort of candy bar, associated with young children and spotted dogs. Clearly, the subjects are not getting their ides from television, as Dr. Faust suggests. As for Dr. Pheelgud's allegations, just because tastes and associations change over time does not mean that there is no connection but rather that there is a connection and that it is mutable. One would not argue that fashion decisions have no ties to personality, clearly what one wears says a lot about who one is, yet these choices also change over time.

The experiments of Dr. Kaloreese and Dr. Rich show Dr. Hogg's belief regarding the relationship between candy bar choice and personality to be true. In fact, their findings serve as scientific proof for the connection. This evidence, along with one's own sense of taste as a function of persona belie the claims of skeptics and demonstrate that Hogg's words are true.

"Though many will fight me on this, and scores of others will cover their eyes and ears to ignore the knowledge I bring,

I will stay on this earth loudly proclaiming what I know to be the truth: as a man lives, so does he eat, and as he chooses candy, so do we know his most private self."

Our Version, With Edits

Here is the version marked with the edits we thought were necessary. Are they the same as your edits? Don't worry if they aren't, but check for differences to see the reasoning behind them.

Candy Bars and Taste

ww
"preference"

Psychology has long posited a connection between the psyche and (taste) in food. The noted professor of food and psychology, (Dr. Ima Hogg,) says, "While many attempt to discover the secrets of the mind through outmoded techniques of psychoanalysis and clinical psychology, the true frontier on which we are discovering the key to personality is by assessment ~~assessing~~ what people eat. Beyond this we cannot hope to go further." (WRITE IN FOOTNOTE FOR HOGG'S STUDY) Hogg's studies relating diet and psychosis went on for over twenty-five years, and they clearly show what any reasonable person has long suspected: (you are what you) eat. Think of the current fad of liquid diet shakes, so appropriate to our American society, caught as it is between the Calvinist puritanism of ~~our~~ its history and the relentless greed and self-indulgence of our current market economy. Consider President Clinton and his fondness for fast food, the food of a person of action, someone ready to lead! (Or) remember the self-destructive habits of the romans, fulfilling the slightest desire with loads of tempting delicacies, then running off to the vomitoria to rid themselves and begin again. (This) demonstrates a clear connection between what one eats and who one is. And indeed, the existence of a connection between food and personality points to the likelihood of a connection between candy bar choice and personality disorder. (Many studies have been done to test this theory and the results of them are here.)

move to beginning of sentence

ment

every

do not use "you"

agreement

this is addition to—use "and" or remove entirely

All these

maybe begin the paper with this?

awk, need better transition sentence

put this later [Much has been written about ~~those~~ *extra* candy bars that combine the various candy elements: nougat, caramel, nuts. The desire for all the things at once, the inability to make any sort of a concrete choice is typical of the boy/man who suffers from the peter pan syndrome, and the combination bar is his candy of choice. ~~This is evidenced on~~
There is both,   *evidence*
~~grounds~~ both academic and emotional. In her ground-breaking treatise on ~~the~~ *this* subject, Dr. Lotta Kaloreese interviewed ~~a group of~~   *unnecessary* 2,500 male participants between the ages of 23 and 55. Of those who
lived what they
said they ~~were either involved or willing to be involved in what they~~ ~~themselves~~ termed a "mature lifestyle," only 19.7% indicated the combination bar, or "Snickers," as their primary candy choice. Of those who professed a longing to return to childhood, or to remain a child indefinitely, an astonishing 78% indicated a strong preference for the Snickers bar as their primary candy choice. (CITE KALORIES'S STUDY) Numerical results this overwhelming cannot
the eternal child
be ignored: Snickers is the bar of ~~those who would be children~~   *repetitive* ~~forever.~~

could begin with this and work up to combination [Another stunning example is the historical references of the caramel. One of the most traditional forms of confection, the caramel is the choice of those who are overly sentimental and prone to emotional outbursts and flights of fancy. Many soft-hearted artists have long called the caramel their favorite, with laudatory remarks often taking the formof song and petry. "Boy, there's nothing a like better than a chocolate bar with caramel in it." (CHECK MLA,DO I NEED TO FOOTNOTE THIS IF I HAVE HIS NAME?) says Barry Manilow, renowned emotional person. This sort of confession is seen

the sentimental

over and over again in memoirs of emotional people. In

writings by John Denver, Sally Field, Tchaikovsky, and other

softies, one can find multiple references to caramel. This

and
happens too frequently to be mere happenstance, one has yet

another reason to believe that there must be some connection

between the formof candy sugar takes, and the type of person

who wants that candy.

Yet another example is apparent in the strong connection

between nut bars and those who love them, the "tough guys," both

male and female. While much has been written on the

connection between nuts of all types and risk-taking daredevils,

including the tie between skydiving and various types of nut

and
brittle, the clearest delineation of candy to personality is

peanuts to machismo. The study was done is most particularly

seen in the desire of river guides, hunters, and rock climbers for

Mr. Goodbar, the peanut chocolate bar. (RICH) Dr. Rich

studied them for
performed his study over two years in all the venues mentioned.

divided the   into three groups
He used three groups among each participants. To the first

arranged to have   for the first group,
group he offered a buffet table at the end of their trips which

ing
contained fruit, chocolate bars of assorted types other than

and
Mr.Goodbars, arranged with the Mr.Goodbars at the back less

reachable part of the table, with the fruit and other candy

toward the front. The participants—94 % of them—reached to

a
the back to get their Mr.Goodbars. Several, 62% of those who

chose the Mr. Goodbar, were heard to grunt the word "Good."

Margin annotations (left):

the connection between

reword

precede this sentence with the other sentence ending in "river guides, hunters, etc."

already understood

Margin annotations (right):

repetition (people, person)

why the fancy word use instance

was commissi to explore well-know

too much

unnecess

arranged so the Mr Goodbars were in a remote,

Not only c this overwhelm majority choose Mr.Goodb but

candy
upon taking the ~~bar.~~ Dr. Rich considered the possibility that

these participants had chosen the bars because they were at the

back and therefore more difficult to reach and therefore a

He used his second group
greater "prize" to these rough and tumble participants, and to

try to weed these out he set up another buffet at which the Mr.

Goodbars were set near the front in easy reach, no challenge at

all. Again an overwhelming majority, 86% this time, chose the

Mr. Goodbar over any other candy. His final group was served

with a mixed buffet on which the candy was arranged every

were
which way, ~~with~~ the results the same. This buffet was, in fact,

picked clean of all peanut related candy, with fruit and other

should   *about*   *d*
footnote candy left strewn ~~apart~~, due, he hypothesizes, to the desire of
this?
"macho" individuals for a hunt for their prey. On returning to

Dr. Rich
his University to organize and publish his findings, he tried a

control group, and offered an audience of 2,000 anthropology

students the same buffet. Only an astonishing 21% chose the

from a selection in which
Mr. Goodbar, and the candy proportions were the same. [There

can be no clearer evidence than this that there is, indeed, a

correlation between candy type and personality.]—————— *to* (A,)
a
section
Scientific reason would lead one to consider whether this *on the*
next
applied to only the nut bar, or the caramel. Recent research in *page*

the chocolate bar field has uncovered some startling findings.

People who purchase the plain chocolate and milk chocolate

bars generally complain of a feeling of a life left unfulfilled, of

feelings and possibilities left unexplored. (WHOEVER)

Similar studies of randomly selected buyers of toffee bars,

including the Heath and the Skör bar indicate that these buyers,

or at least 89% of these buyers, can be classified as suffering

from superiority complexes, defined as the strong belief that

do not
personalize   they are better than the rest of us) The compelling evidence

linking the lover of coconut bars and the psychopath only

cements the bond.

      Nevertheless, There are many in both the scientific and confectionery

doubt the / community who protest that chocolate bar preference is merely a
detractors

matter of personal taste, and (hence) unrelated to any personality   *pompous?*
                                                      change

quirks. Most notable among these groups are Dr. Faust and Dr.   *introduce*
                                                        him later,
Pheelgud. Dr. Faust notes that much as the experiments have   *with his*
                                                        theory

done to set up control groups, the studies done have not covered

a wide enough expanse of the population. FOOTNOTE? OR

LATER ON? In fact, all the studies, he notes, have been done in
                                    companies
the United States where the candy bars advertise their images
                        he maintains
via television commercials. Thus it is these media images of the

bars that people respond to, not the bars themselves. Dr.
                another opponent of candy and personality theory,
Pheelgud notes in his book, [Candy Bars and Personality: There's   *italics*

No Connection,] that candy bars and what goes in them changes

over time, for instance licorice is not nearly as popular as it was

in the early forties. PHEELGUD This change over time

indicates to her that there is no real correlation, because that

would indicate a change in human personality type within the

space of a decade, and this she considers unlikely.

too much?

While these doctors are to be commended for their (dogged) attempts

to discover the truth, their arguments cannot withstand scientific

scrutiny. Dr. Faust is correct in noting that the studies have been done

for the most part in the United States, but he ignores the important

as well as

Swiss chocolate series of the Kiss Institute, and the Mousse inquiries of

need to

have a   the Academe Francais, AF As for his contention that television affects

sentence of the subjects ability to respond in an unbiased manner toward the candy

explanation

for what   bar, he forgets that the images subjects respond to are not those

these   projected by the candy company. For instance, as discussed earlier, Mr.

studies are

and what   Goodbar is loved by those who attempt to prove their prowess in sports

they show   and outdoor pursuits, yet the advertised image of Mr. Goodbar is as a

friendly "fun" sort of candy bar, associated with young children and

a

spotted dogs. Clearly, the subjects are not getting their ideas from

television, as Dr. Faust suggests. As for Dr. Pheelgud's allegations, just

because tastes and associations change over time does not mean that

it implies,   *ital?*

there is no connection but rather that there (is) a connection and that it is

mutable. One would not argue that fashion decisions have no ties to

personality, clearly what one wears says a lot about who one is, yet

these choices also change over time.

The experiments of Dr. Kaloreese and Dr. Rich show Dr. Hogg's

belief regarding the relationship between candy bar choice and

decide—

personality (personality) to be true. In fact, their findings serve as scientific proof for

or

personality the connection. This evidence, along with one's own sense of taste as a

disorder   function of persona belie the claims of skeptics and demonstrate that

Hogg's words are true.

"Though many will fight me on this, and scores of others will cover

ir

the eyes and ears to ignore the knowledge I bring, I will stay on this

earth loudly proclaiming what I know to be the truth: as a man lives, so

does he eat, and as he chooses candy, so do we know his most private

self."

Once you have made all the edits, both organizational and stylistic, you are ready to put your paper into its final stages, complete with reference and format specifications. This work is mostly mechanical, but does necessitate that you pay close attention to minute details. The end is in sight, but don't let that allow you a sloppy finish.

STEP 8: CREATE A BIBLIOGRAPHY

A bibliography is the list of references used in the writing of a paper. Compile your bibliography according to the rules given by your teacher, professor, or *The MLA Handbook for Writers of Research Papers, Theses, and Dissertations.*

STEP 9: TITLE YOUR PAPER

Finally, when the rest of the paper is sitting on your desk all clean and edited with bibliography, you can create a title. For some reason, academic papers tend to have titles with colons in them.

Spiderman: Arachnid or Anarchist?

Stalin, Hitler, and Mussolini:
People I'm Glad I Didn't Know

And so forth. Your title should indicate the subject of your paper in a pithy manner, and, if possible, be eye-catching. Don't be afraid to have some fun with this; it's the part of your paper your teacher sees first and should be as interesting as you can make it.

STEP 10: TYPE UP A FINAL DRAFT

Sometimes You Feel Like A Nut, Sometimes You Don't:

Candy Bars and the Psychology of Taste

by Tim

Psychology has long posited a connection between the psyche and food preferences. Noted professor of food and psychology Dr. Ima Hogg says, "While many attempt to discover the secrets of the mind through outmoded techniques of psychoanalysis and clinical psychology, the true frontier on which we are discovering the key to personality is an assessment of what people eat."[1] Hogg's studies relating diet and psychosis went on for over twenty-five years, and they clearly show what every reasonable person has long suspected: one is what one eats. Think of the current fad of liquid diet shakes, so appropriate to American society, caught as it is between the Calvinist puritanism of its history and the relentless greed and self-indulgence of its current market economy. Consider President Clinton and his fondness for fast food, the food of a person of action, someone ready to lead! Remember the self-destructive habits of the Romans, fulfilling the slightest desire with loads of tempting delicacies, then running off to the vomitoria to rid themselves and begin again. All these demonstrate a clear connection between what one eats and who one is. Further, the existence of a connection between food and personality points to the likelihood of a connection between candy bar choice and personality disorder.

---

[1] Ima Hogg, Let's Eat Some More (New York: Glutton & Sons, 1994), p. 107.

This theory has been tested time and time again, and the results of these tests coincide: there is a connection. One of the earliest such studies explored the historical references of the caramel. Perhaps the most traditional form of confection, the caramel is the choice of those who are overly sentimental and prone to emotional outbursts and flights of fancy. Many soft-hearted artists have long called the caramel their favorite, with laudatory remarks often taking the form of song and poetry. "Boy, there's nothing I like better than a chocolate bar with caramel in it."[2] says Barry Manilow, renowned emotional person. This sort of confession is seen over and over again in memoirs of emotional people. In writings by John Denver, Sally Field, Tchaikovsky, and other softies, one can find multiple references to caramel. This happens too frequently to be mere happenstance, yet another reason to believe that there must be some connection between the form of candy sugar takes, and the type of person who wants that candy.

Much has also been written about candy bars that combine the various candy elements: nougat, caramel, nuts. The desire for all things at once, the inability to make any sort of a concrete choice is typical of the boy/man who suffers from the Peter Pan syndrome, and the combination bar is his candy of choice. There is both academic and emotional evidence. In her ground-breaking treatise on this subject, Dr. Lotta Kaloreese interviewed 2,500

[2] Barry Manilow, Notes on a Sentimental Life (Hawaii: Soft Hearts & Company, 1993) p.21.

male participants between the ages of 23 and 55. Of those who said they lived what they termed a "mature lifestyle," only 19.7% indicated the combination bar, or "Snickers," as their primary candy choice. Of those who professed a longing to return to childhood or to remain a child indefinitely, an astonishing 78% indicated a strong preference for the Snickers bar as their primary candy choice.[3] Numerical results this overwhelming cannot be ignored: Snickers is the bar of the eternal child.

Yet another example is apparent in the strong connection between nut bars and those who love them, the "tough guys," both male and female. While much has been written on the connection between nuts of all types and risk-taking daredevils, including the tie between skydiving and various types of nut brittle, the clearest instance of candy's connection to personality is the tie between peanuts and machismo. A study was commissioned to examine the common desire among river guides, hunters, and rock climbers for the Mr. Goodbar, a chocolate bar with peanuts.[4] Dr. Rich divided the participants into three groups and studied them over two years. He arranged to have a buffet table for the first group, containing fruit and chocolate bars of assorted types, including Mr. Goodbars. He designed the buffet so the Mr. Goodbars were in a remote, less reachable part of the table. The partici-

---

[3] Lotta Kaloreese, "Men Who Would Be Children" in Experiments in Chocolate, (Pennsylvania: Bar Press, 1991) pp. 32-45.

[4] Tu Rich, Peanuts And Machismo (Texas: Men Don't Press, 1993) p.10.

pants—94% of them—reached to the back to get a Mr. Goodbar. Not only did this overwhelming majority select Mr. Goodbar, but 62% of those who chose the Mr. Goodbar were heard to grunt the word "Good" upon taking the candy. Dr. Rich considered the possibility that these participants had chosen the bars because they were at the back and more difficult to reach, therefore a greater "prize" to these rough-and-tumble participants. He used his second group to try to weed these out. He set up another buffet at which the Mr. Goodbars were set near the front in easy reach, no challenge at all. Again an overwhelming majority, 86% this time, chose Mr. Goodbar over any other candy. His final group was served with a mixed buffet on which the candy was arranged every which way, and the results were the same. This buffet was, in fact, picked clean of all peanut-related candy, with fruit and other candy left strewn about, due, he hypothesized, to the desire of "macho" individuals for a hunt for their prey. On returning to his university to organize and publish his findings, Dr. Rich examined a control group. He offered an audience of 2,000 anthropology students the same buffet. Only 21% chose the Mr. Goodbar from a selection in which the candy proportions were the same.

Scientific curiosity would lead one to consider whether this connection between personality and preference applied only to the nut bar and the caramel. Recent research in the chocolate bar field has uncovered some startling findings. People who purchase plain chocolate and milk chocolate bars generally complain of a feeling of a life left unfulfilled, of feelings and possibilities left unexplored.[5] Similar studies of randomly selected buyers of toffee bars, including the Heath and the Skör bar, indicate that at least 89% of these buyers suffer from superiority complexes, defined as the strong belief that they are better than the rest of the population. The compelling evidence linking the lover of coconut bars and the psychopath only cements the bond. There can be no clearer evidence than this that there is, indeed, a correlation between candy type and personality.

Nevertheless, there are many in both the scientific and confectionery community who protest that chocolate bar preference is merely a matter of personal taste, and therefore unrelated to any personality quirks. Notable among these is Dr. Faust. Dr. Faust notes that, much as the experimenters have tried to set up control groups, none of the studies have covered a wide enough expanse of the population.[6] Furthermore, Dr. Faust adds, the studies have all been conducted in the United States, where the candy bar companies advertise their images via television commercials. Thus, he maintains, people in the United States respond to these media images, not to the bars themselves. Dr. Pheelgud, another opponent of candy-personality theory, notes in her book *Candy Bars and Personality: There's No Connection* that candy

---

[5] Hy Phat, "The Life I Could Have Had: Plain Chocolate and the Repressed" in <u>Watchamacallit and Aphasia: A Journal of Chocolate and Mental Health,</u> (Arizona: Bench Press, 1992).
[6] Goethe Faust, "I'd Sell My Soul to Publish a Book About Candy" in <u>Dubious Arguments Review No. 31</u> (New York: Hell University Press, 1990) pp. 14-23.

bars, and what goes into them, change over time. For instance licorice is not nearly as popular as it was in the early forties.[7] This change over time indicates to her that there is no real correlation, because that would indicate a change in human personality type within the space of a century, and this she considers unlikely.

While Faust and Pheelgud are to be commended for their dogged attempts to discover the truth, their arguments cannot withstand scientific scrutiny. Dr. Faust is correct in noting that the studies have been conducted for the most part in the United States, but he ignores the important Swiss chocolate series of the Kiss Institute, as well as the Mousse inquiries of the Académie francaise.[8] The Kiss Institute found the same superiority connection referred to earlier, displayed by over 500 participants from France, Switzerland, and Germany. The Mousse inquiries provided convincing evidence for the claim that various forms of mousse can be used in the treatment of many types of neuroses, establishing another clear connection between the psyche and chocolate. As for Dr. Faust's contention that television affects the subject's ability to respond in an unbiased manner toward the candy bar, he does not consider that the images projected by the candy company are unrelated to the interests and aspirations of the candy

---

[7] I. Pheelgud, Candy Bars and Personality: There's No Connection (New York: Skeptics & Company, 1988) pp. 34-35.

[8] Swiss Miss, The Mousse Inquiries (Switzerland: Braids & Company, 1962).

devotees. For instance, as discussed earlier, Mr. Goodbar is loved by those who attempt to prove their prowess in sports and outdoor pursuits, yet the advertised image of Mr. Goodbar is as a friendly "fun" sort of candy bar, associated with young children and spotted dogs. Clearly, the subjects are not getting their ideas from television, though Dr. Faust believes otherwise. As for Dr. Pheelgud's allegations, just because tastes and associations change over time does not mean that there is no connection between the two. It implies, rather, that there *is* a connection and it is mutable. One would not argue that fashion decisions have no ties to personality, clearly what one wears says a lot about who one is, yet these choices also change over time.

The experiments of Dr. Kaloreese and Dr. Rich show Dr. Hogg's belief regarding the relationship between candy bar choice and personality to be true. In fact, their findings serve as scientific proof for the connection. This evidence, along with one's own sense of taste as a function of persona, belie the claims of skeptics and demonstrate the truth of Hogg's words.

"Though many will fight me on this, and scores of others will cover their eyes and ears to ignore the knowledge I bring, I will stay on this earth loudly proclaiming what I know to be the truth: as a man lives, so does he eat, and as he chooses candy, so do we know his most private self."[9]

---

[9] Hogg, p.72.

BIBLIOGRAPHY

Faust, Goethe. "I'd Sell My Soul to Publish a Book About Candy" Dubious Arguments Review No. 31. (1990), 14-23.

Hogg, Ima. Let's Eat Some More. New York: Glutton & Sons, 1994.

Kaloreese, Lotta. "Men Who Would Be Children." In Experiments in Chocolate. Ed. Russell Upsom Grubb. Pennsylvania: Bar Press, 1991.

Manilow, Barry. Notes on a Sentimental Life. Hawaii: Soft Hearts & Company, 1993.

Miss, Swiss. The Mousse Inquiries. Switzerland: Braids & Company, 1962.

Phat, Hy. "The Life I Could Have Had: Plain Chocolate and the Repressed." In Watchamacallit and Aphasia: An Introduction to Chocolate and Mental Health. Ed. Roland Butter. Arizona: Bench Press, 1992.

Pheelgud, I. Candy Bars And Personality: There's No Connection. New York: Skeptics & Co. 1988.

Rich, Tu. Peanuts And Machismo: I Know They Are Connected. Texas: Men Don't Press, 1993.

Whipt, I. M. "An Important Study." Nougat Quarterly, 103 (1987), 12-34.

COMMON RESEARCH PAPER PITFALLS

ORGANIZATIONAL SWAMP

The organizing process may take you quite a while and there is the temptation to say to yourself, "Oh my god I've been working on this paper organization for four hours and I haven't written a thing! I should be killed." Relax. Thinking through your paper is an important step of writing.

But. Don't get caught in the endless-note-taking trap. A pleasant rule of thumb: the length of your notes should not exceed the length of your paper. If you find yourself buying a second package of 100 index cards, you've gone overboard; reign yourself in, organize the cards, and start writing.

WRITING AS YOU GO

Finish your research before you start writing, because you never know if something you find will prove your thesis wrong or right. The research process helps you know what you want to write. Writing before your research is finished is like constructing a building before the blueprint has been drawn.

WAITING TOO LONG

With an organized outlook and meticulous research you can write a term paper in less time than you might think. Nevertheless, you should still allow yourself at least one week for every five pages. Trying to write the paper in one night will, in most cases, ensure that you produce a paper that is poorly written and conceptually crippled. You've probably heard of the all-nighter, as in, "I stayed up all night and wrote the whole paper in five hours and then I got an A." But the martyr complex that leads people to lose sleep and then brag about it as though they had done something intelligent is an irritating collegiate romanticization that most everyone would be better off avoiding. If you know you are the type to procrastinate, set up a written schedule giving yourself due dates for your research, your outlines, your first five pages, etc. Then give it to someone who you trust will bug you enough to remind you but not enough so you will never forgive her.

PERFECTION

"What?" you say, "Perfection a pitfall?"

Here's the situation: If you try to make every sentence that you write perfect as you write it, the odds are that you will never get your paper written. You have the opportunity to edit your paper once it is written. The purpose of the paper is to present your thesis and your research, not to write the perfect sentence. Get your paper written in rough draft and *then* attempt perfection, or you will end up writing the first sentence for the rest of your life.

FUDGING RESEARCH

Don't take credit for someone else's work, fake footnotes, or fake research. It's wrong, and you will get caught. Clear enough?

PADDING

It is tempting, sometimes, to blab on for hours because you feel your paper has to achieve a certain length. Say what you mean to say and no more; any unnecessary sentences will only weaken your paper. The number of pages suggested for an assignment is just that, "suggestions." Your paper should be long enough to cover your topic, and once you have covered it, finish. Pieces that don't belong will stick out and destabilize the structure you have invested so much time in building.

SPECIFICS

Since term papers are all about research, you must indicate the sources of your research within your paper. This is done with footnotes (or endnotes), references within the text, and a bibliography. For basic formats on reference work, use whichever stylistic guidelines your teacher gives you. If your teacher does not give a specific recommendation, use *The MLA Handbook for Writers of Research Papers, Theses, and Dissertations.*

There are some rules to follow when including references within a paper.

QUOTATIONS SHOULD BE COPIED EXACTLY, AND REFERENCED

If you must shorten a quotation, indicate that sections were removed by using the ellipses, those three dots ". . ." which translate to "Something has been omitted here."

QUOTATIONS OF FEWER THAN FOUR TYPED LINES

These are put in the same format as the paper, within quotation marks, and introduced by a comma or a colon. Quotations of four typed lines or longer are also introduced by a comma or a colon, but are set off from the text by triple spacing, and indented five lines on either side; often they are also single-spaced.

FOOTNOTES AND ENDNOTES

They are ordered references indicated by a superscript number after a paraphrase or quotation that is not your own.[1] These references should be used only when necessary. Useless quotes used to pad the length will be spotted, and notes that have been fractured to provide a higher number of notes will weaken your writing. Footnotes are written at the bottom of the page on which the reference appears, endnotes are given on a separate page at the end of the paper. Footnotes and endnotes serve the same purpose; the format you use depends on your teacher's preference. If you are using a typewriter, endnotes are much easier because you are not forced to save room at the bottom of the page. If you use a computer either is equally easy. Notes are consecutively numbered and are placed at the end of the quote or paraphrase, after the punctuation. Following is the standard form as pronounced by the Modern Language Association.

---

[1] It looks just like this.

In the body of your paper:

> As some people do not know how else to survive in New York, many social experts make helpful suggestions: "If actual friends are not within your grasp, may I suggest that you take a cue from your favorite celebrity and consider investing in a really good entourage."[2]

Followed by the note, either at the bottom of the page or the end of your paper:

[2]Fran Lebowitz, "Pointers For Pets," in *Social Studies* (New York: Random House, 1977), p. 61.

If you continue with references to the same book you can repeat the author's last name and show the new page.

[3]Lebowitz, pp. 117–118.

If you have used two different books by the same author you can repeat the author's last name, and the title or an abbreviation of the title, and then the page number(s). Like this:

[4]Lebowitz, *Metropolitan Life*, p. 56.

There are endless variations on note format, for articles in periodicals, books with multiple authors, and so on. The basic rule is that the author's name is given first; the book title is underlined, unless you can italicize; an article or section of a book is put in quotation marks; and the publication information is given. *The MLA Handbook for Writers of Research Papers, Theses, and Dissertations* is the definitive source for these formats. Obviously you should try to use the correct format whenever possible, but when in doubt try to remember that the point of footnotes and endnotes is to ascertain that credit has been given. As long as you do that, you can relax.

REFERENCES WITHIN THE TEXT

These are used only in papers with very few references. (*MLA Handbook*, 1977 ed. [New York: Modern Language Association, 1977], p. 94.) Basically, include all the information you would have written in the footnote, as we just did.

BIBLIOGRAPHY

A bibliography is a list of all the works used in compiling a research paper. If you have used a book or article for information, it belongs in your bibliography, even if you have not directly cited it. Do not list books you did not use, no matter how fancy you want to appear. If you have used footnotes or endnotes you should list the works in alphabetical order without numbers. If you have used references within the text, (see directly preceding paragraph) number your entries.

Bibliography entries are constructed differently from footnotes. Here is what a bibliography should look like:

Lebowitz, Fran. *Social Studies*. New York: Random House, 1977.

Why is it so different? We don't know, but this is what is expected, so this is what you shall do.

TITLE

Don't underline, capitalize, or do anything else fancy to the title. You can have a title page if you want one, but it is not necessary.

PAGE NUMBERS

Do not count the title page, if you include one, in the page count. The page count starts on the first page but you don't write down the page number until the second page. This is because we assume the reader knows that the first page he is reading is, in fact, the first page.

UNDERLINING

Titles of books, plays, and long poems get italics. If you have no italics, underline. Titles of shorter pieces get put in quotation marks.

AND THUS. . .

Research papers aren't so terrible, they just call for a concerted plan of attack and some scheduling. Writing them is no more difficult than writing any essay. If you ever get stuck and don't know what to write next, ask yourself, "What am I trying to say?" and write that down. That is the surest way to clear, direct communication through writing.

BOOK LIST

These books are not generally fun to read, except *The Elements of Style*, but they contain useful information for research paper writers like yourself.

Guide to Reference Books, American Library Association.
MLA Handbook for Writers of Research Papers, Theses, and Dissertations, Modern Language Association.
William Strunk and E. B. White, *The Elements of Style*, Macmillan.

CHAPTER 8

Professional Letters

T here will be a time in your life when you must write some sort of professional letter. This may be in connection with a job or a request or a recommendation, but the time will come. You must be prepared!

FORMAT

SALUTATION
Begin by saying "hello," and identifying yourself.

BODY OF THE LETTER
Explain why you are writing.

ADIEU
Offer warm words of closing, unless you are writing the "Outraged Letter" (see end of chapter).

HOW TO WRITE A PROFESSIONAL LETTER, WITH DUNCAN

A letter you will be proud of, like any other piece of writing, requires multiple drafts.

STEP 1: KNOW YOUR PURPOSE
The first thing you want to get straight is deciding exactly what you want to say.

> Duncan is applying for a job and needs to include a cover letter along with his resume. He has met the person in charge of hiring, and wants both to remind her of their meeting, and sound warm, witty, and competent. He writes down on his note pad:

I know you from the Texas conference on UFOs, please give me this job—I'm good at it, I have experience, I am eager to work for you. I'm not desperate either.

These are his notes for a first draft.

STEP 2: THE FIRST DRAFT

Clarify your intent, and put your notes in letter form. Write freely and easily, for next you will edit. Try to keep your tone restrained and professional, and bear your audience in mind. Also, if you have any sort of connection via a friend or colleague who knows the recipient, say so. This greatly affects the outcome. But beware, avoid dropping the name of someone hated by the boss, if you can help it.

STEP 3: EDIT THE MONSTER

Edit the following letter. You want the result to be clear and impressive. Duncan's ideas should be apparent—your job here is to ensure they are clearly expressed in a professional manner. Also, most letters requesting work or interviews should be kept to one page, if at all possible. You may separate the letter into separate paragraphs if you find it necessary, or add sentences that crystallize the meaning. As usual, the edits we have made are on the copy that follows, and a final draft incorporates these edits as well as other rewrites.

Dear Ms. Hankshaw,

Maybe you remember me from last year's conference on aliens. I am Duncan Bock and I ran the booth on the Martian, friend or foe? I am enclosing my resume to be considered for the position of assistant commander in charge of alien visitors in your alien welcoming army.

I look forward to hearing from you.

Love, Duncan

Edited Version

Dear Ms. Hankshaw,

expand on the meeting to jog her memory

Maybe you remember me from last year's conference on aliens. [I am Duncan Bock] and I ran the booth ~~on the~~ Martian, friend or

list credential

punctuation

capitalize title

foe? I am enclosing my resume to be considered for the

position of assistant commander in charge of alien visitors in

your alien welcoming army.

why?

[I look forward to hearing from you.]

not her response

Sincerely,
~~Love,~~ Duncan

Enclosures?

STEP 4: FINAL FORM

The last step is to put the letter in its final form. If at all possible, try to find someone else to read the letter and point out any errors. Workplaces are far less tolerant of errors than are academic institutions. Pay close attention to matters of form because the look of a business letter is easily as important as its content. You must use clean paper, no wrinkles, stains, or tears. You must allow no mistakes of any kind. Check carefully. Notice on this final draft the changes that were made to accommodate edits for tone and style on the previous drafts.

Duncan Smith
123 Freak Street
Hole, New York 11111
June 5, 1994

Ms. Hankshaw
Commander of Forces
Aliens Are Coming Soon, Inc.
2435 Outuvmy Way
Los Angeles, California 90210

Dear Ms. Hankshaw:

I had the privilege of meeting you at the 1993 Conference on
Alien Life where I ran the booth, "Martian: Friend or Foe?" I
enjoyed speaking with you regarding the future of our extraterrestrial communications systems.

I am writing to be considered for the position of Assistant
Commander in Charge of Welcoming Alien Visitors. I have worked
welcoming various extraterrestrial visitors all over California and
the southwest, receiving the prestigious E.T. award, among others.
I have enjoyed this work and the people and aliens I have been
privileged to encounter. Your project, as well as this position
in it, sounds extremely exciting, and I look forward to finding
out more about both.

I appreciate the time you've taken in this matter, and I will call
soon to set up an interview appointment.

Sincerely,

Duncan Smith

Duncan Smith

Enc. Resume

THE OUTRAGED LETTER

FROM "THE LETTERS OF JEFFREY FLANDERS AND TIP-TOP UTILITY"

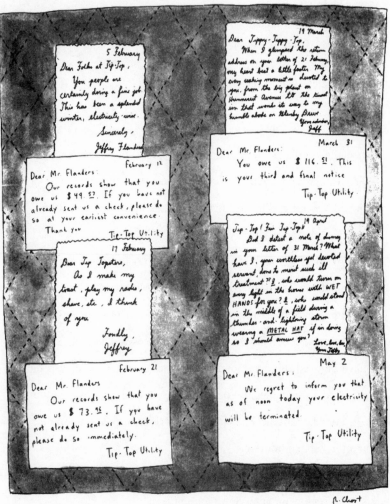

Has someone done you wrong? Did the gas company overcharge you? Did your toaster explode? Does your compact disc player make all singers sound as though they have inhaled helium? Fear not, you have recourse. You can write the "Outraged Letter."

Without doubt, the righteously angry letter is one of the most enjoyable pieces to write. You are given the opportunity for high drama and justified fury; you can vent any anger you may have stored up over time in response to slights and snubs. You can prevail over the powers of evil.

FORMAT

ADDRESS
Identify yourself and to whom you wish to speak.

BODY OF LETTER
Describe the unfortunate event the letter refers to in the most specific terms possible.

CLOSING
Indicate how you want the company or person to redress your grievances.

HOW TO WRITE A TRULY FURIOUS LETTER, WITH CONNIE

STEP 1: WRITE DOWN WHO YOU ARE AND WHAT HAPPENED
To begin, you must inform the recipient in explicit detail exactly what has made you angry. Only then can you wreak your terrible vengeance. Bear in mind, though, that even in an angry letter it is advisable to be polite, if chilly. No matter what your personal feelings, obscenities and ranting are ill-advised.

"Well," said Connie, "they think they can get away with giving me a faulty doll house. So what if I stole it from my niece? So what if I'm forty, and, some would say, too old for dolls? Well, it's payback time." She takes out a pad and writes, "The stove in my doll house with the tiny revolving turkey didn't work. I called and called and called and was not treated well. It's rude and unfair.

> Sent letter 1/7, called Mr. Babyface 1/14, received 2nd letter 1/24, called 1/24, 1/25, 1/28 received message, February 2nd called twice in the morning as I was told to, paid a total of $228.69 to his company. CEO of Company is Ms. L.I. Dahl.

STEP 2: THE ROUGH DRAFT

Compile your notes into a rough first draft. You should follow the form given on page 129. Explain any previous contact you have had with the person to whom you are writing. Then, in as much detail as possible, describe how you have been wronged. Keep the letter in clear chronological order.

STEP 3: EDIT

Edit the following rough draft of an outraged letter, with the aim of a restrained, polite, outraged letter. Then, compare with the edited version on the following page.

2/7/94

Mr. Babyface:

Two months ago I sent you a letter detailing the problems I was experiencing with my rotating turkey in my doll house oven on my doll house model #25143. I informed you that I had received in return a letter from your company noting that I would *not* be compensated for my troubles. When I discussed that letter with you on the phone you said, "It's a mistake. The department made a mistake and about 6 million customers got one of those letters. Just send it to me and I'll take care of it. I will get you registered as a customer with a complaint and you will be reimbursed for your turkey, as well as your pain and suffering." I sent it to you and assumed that there would be no problem.

Two weeks ago, January 24, I received another notice that I would not be receiving reimbursement for my pain and suffering, and that I owed for the repair to the turkey as well as interest on the repair bill. I then called your office, Monday, January 24. No response. I called Tuesday, Wednesday, etc. On Friday at 5 p.m. I got a message from you, but of course I was unable to reach you as your office had closed. I called every day of the next week. I got one more call from you saying you would be reachable on Wednesday February 2, in the morning. I called at 8:55 a.m. and 9:30 a.m. Either no one answered or I was told you were not in. I called again every day, sometimes twice a day, and was told you were out in "the field."

That may in fact be the case, but there are phones in other places. I was given to understand that you were dealing with important clients. Mr. Babyface, I am an important client too. While I was not pleased that my rotating turkey did not function, I am even more offended by the way you have responded to my attempts to address the situation. I paid you $200 for the doll house and a lifetime of servicing and you did it poorly. You rude idiot, I will not be treated this way!! You can forget any other business from me you idiotic dolt. I expect you to pay the $22.69 in interest I was assessed, and I expect you to return my initial payment of $200 which, I think you will agree, you did not earn.

Edited First Draft

2/7/94

Mr. Babyface:

Two months ago I sent you a letter detailing the problems I was

redundant   experiencing with⟨my⟩rotating turkey in⟨my⟩doll house oven on⟨my⟩

doll house model #25143. I informed you that I had received

unnecessary   ⟨in return⟩a letter from your company noting that I would⟨not⟩be   *no italics*

compensated for my troubles. When I discussed that letter with you

on the phone you said, "It's a mistake. The department made a

mistake and about 6 million customers got one of those letters. Just

send it to me and I'll take care of it. I will get you registered as a

customer with a complaint and you will be reimbursed for your

turkey, as well as your pain and suffering." I sent it to you and

assumed that there would be no problem.

Two weeks ago, January 24, I received another notice that I

would not be receiving reimbursement for my pain and suffering,

and that I owed for the repair to the turkey as well as interest on the

repair bill. I then called your office, Monday, January 24. No

response. I called Tuesday, Wednesday, etc. On Friday at 5 p.m. I

got a message from you, but of course I was unable to reach you as

your office had closed. I called every day of the next week. I got

one more call from you saying you would be reachable on

Wednesday, February 2, in the morning. I called at 8:55 a.m. and

Both   9:30 a.m.⟨Either⟩no one answered⟨or⟩I was told you were not in. I
happened

called again every day, sometimes twice a day, and was told you

were out in "the field."

That may in fact be the case, but there are phones in other

places. I was given to understand that you were dealing with

important clients. Mr. Babyface, I am an important client too.

While I was not pleased that my rotating turkey did not function, I

am even more offended by the way you have responded to my

he did not attempts to address the situation. I paid you $200 for the doll house
do it at all!

and a lifetime of servicing and you did it poorly. You rude idiot, I   *calm down!*
                                                                              detail
will not be treated this way!! You can forget any other business   *rational*
                                                                              retaliation
from me you idiotic dolt. I expect you to pay the $22.69 in interest

I was assessed, and I expect you to return my initial payment of   *not just*
                                                                             him, the
$200 which, I think you will agree, you did not earn.   *whole*
                                                                             company

Annotate cc: CEO

STEP 4: FINAL DRAFT

The final draft of a letter must be as perfect as you can make it.
Any outbursts must be deleted, and any typos, spelling errors or
grammatical mistakes must be rectified. Your letter should, while
maintaining an icy yet polite tone, explain the problem and clarify
how you would like the recipient to address the problem.

Final Draft

Connie Smith

123 Righteous Place

New York, New York 11111

February 7, 1994

Mr. Otto Babyface

Cute Doll Houses Inc.

666 Devils Way

Too Cute Stuff, Hell 66666

Mr. Babyface:

Two months ago I sent you a letter detailing the problems I was experiencing with the rotating turkey in my doll house oven on doll house model #25143. I informed you that I had received a letter from your company noting that I would not be compensated for my troubles. When I discussed that letter with you on the phone you said, "It's a mistake. The department made a mistake and about 6 million customers got one of those letters. Just send it to me and I'll take care of it. I will get you registered as a customer with a complaint and you will be reimbursed for your turkey, as well as your pain and suffering." I sent it to you and assumed you would take care of the problem.

Two weeks ago, January 24, I received another notice that I would not receive reimbursement for my pain and suffering, and that I owed for the repair to the turkey as well as interest on the repair bill. I then called your office, Monday, January

24. No response. I called Tuesday, Wednesday, etc. No response. On Friday at 5 p.m. I got a message from you, but of course I was unable to reach you as your office had closed. I called every day of the next week. I got one more call from you saying you would be reachable on Wednesday, February 2, in the morning. I called at 8:55 a.m. and 9:30 a.m. First no one answered, then I was told you were not in. I called again every day, sometimes twice a day, and was told you were out in "the field."

That may in fact be the case, but there are phones in other places. I was given to understand that you were dealing with important clients. Mr. Babyface, I am an important client too. While I was not pleased that my rotating turkey did not function, I am even more offended by the way you have responded to my attempts to address the situation. I paid you $200 for a functioning doll house and a lifetime of servicing, and received neither. You ignored my phone calls. This sort of discourtesy is unacceptable, and I am alerting all the people to whom I had recommended your firm, as well as the man who had originally recommended you to me. I expect you to pay the $22.89 in interest I was assessed, and I expect you to return my payment of $200 which, I think you will agree, your company has not earned.

Connie Smith

Connie Smith

cc: Ms. Liv Ing Doll, CEO

Notice that in the final version of the letter Connie expresses her concerns as well as her outrage, but never allows herself to resort to vulgarity or shrieking. She also informs Mr. Babyface—Otto to us—of the ways he can fix the problems. These are the goals of any outraged letter.

COMMON PITFALLS FOR ALL TYPES OF LETTERS

GENTLEMEN

There is little that will make a woman more furious then receiving a letter addressed to "Gentlemen." If you do not know exactly to whom you are writing, use "To whom it may concern," "Members of the board," or some other term that is not gender-specific.

LOVE

You may be a lovely warmhearted person, but you must try to restrain yourself. There are many ways to sign off on a business letter, but "Love" is not among them.

GOING ON AND ON

Get to the point as soon as common decency allows, and then sign off. Recipients will appreciate your brevity for its form as well as the respite it allows them.

OBSCENITIES & OUTBURSTS

Your message will be relayed much more effectively with restrained anger than with shocking expletives. If someone reads a letter describing them as a part of the body that does not often see the light of day, they generally discard that letter.

EMBARRASSING FAMILIARITY

If you don't know the person to whom you are writing, and even if you know them slightly, only be familiar to the degree that is warranted by your association. Nobody wants someone she doesn't really know making overly personal comments and asking intrusive questions. Remember, discretion is the better part of valor.

LACK OF CONTROL

While it is helpful to be enthusiastic, particularly if your letter concerns a job request or the like, an overall excited tone tends to make you appear desperate. Allow writing to convey your ideas; your writing itself is not meant to be the focus.

SPECIFICS

Professional letters should always contain both your name and address and the addressee's name and address. Your name and address should be at the top, flush with the right margin, along with the date, and the addressee's information should be below your name, flush with the left margin. After the addressee's information, double space and then begin your salutation, "Dear Ms. Prynne," or whatever it is, followed by a comma or a colon—either is fine. As discussed previously (paragraphing chapter, pages 26–27), you can paragraph by either indenting or by double spacing between paragraphs. Professional letters generally have the double space between paragraphs.

Your sign-off should be on the lower left of the letter, followed by a comma, then two double spaces are left empty. This is so you can sign your name with an appropriate flourish. After the signature space, also on the lower left, you should type out your name, in full.

If necessary, extra markings can alert the recipient of the letter to any enclosures (Enc.) or other copies sent that may be of interest to them (cc: Mr. Ed). The "cc" stands for the long-ago carbon copy, and should be marked if you want the recipient to know you have sent the same letter to his boss, or someone else within the same company.

Connie Smith

123 Righteous Place

New York, New York 11111

February 7, 1994

ADDRESS

Mr. Otto Babyface

Cute Doll Houses Inc.

666 Devils Way

Too Cute Stuff, Hell 66666

SALUTATION

Mr. Babyface:

BODY

Two months ago I sent you a letter detailing the problems I was experiencing with the rotating turkey in my doll house oven on doll house model #25143. I informed you that I had received a letter from your company noting that I would not be compensated for my troubles. When I discussed that letter with you on the phone you said, "It's a mistake. The department made a mistake and about 6 million customers got one of those letters. Just send it to me and I'll take care of it. I will get you registered as a customer with a complaint and you will be reimbursed for your turkey, as well as your pain and suffering." I sent it to you and assumed you would take care of the problem.

Two weeks ago, January 24, I received another notice that I would not receive reimbursement for my pain and suffering, and that I owed for the repair to the turkey as well as interest on the repair bill. I then called your office on Monday, January 24. No response. I called Tuesday, Wednesday, etc. No response.

On Friday at 5 p.m. I got a message from you, but of course I was unable to reach you as your office had closed. I called every day of the next week. I got one more call from you saying you would be reachable on Wednesday, February 2, in the morning. I called at 8:55 a.m. and 9:30 a.m. First no one answered, then I was told you were not in. I called again every day, sometimes twice a day, and was told you were out in "the field."

That may in fact be the case, but there are phones in other places. I was given to understand that you were dealing with important clients. Mr. Babyface, I am an important client too. While I was not pleased that my rotating turkey did not function, I am even more offended by the way you have responded to my attempts to address the situation. I paid you $200 for a functioning doll house and a lifetime of servicing, and received neither. You ignored my phone calls. This sort of discourtesy is unacceptable, and I am alerting all the people to whom I had recommended your firm, as well as the man who had originally recommended you to me. I expect you to pay the $22.89 in interest I was assessed, and I expect you to return my payment of $200 which, I think you will agree, your company has not earned.

Connie Smith

cc: Ms. Liv Ing Doll, CEO

And Thus...

Though many believe letters have gone the way of the horse and carriage, a well-written letter can have more impact than a million phone messages. Your letter will allow you to present yourself clearly and cogently, and if you take the time to craft and check it, can display your eloquence far better than a conversation. So practice; this skill will serve you well your entire life.

Book List

Some of these books contain letters and some contain instructions on how to write letters. All believe in the letter as a powerful tool. See what you can learn from them.

Choderlos de Laclos, *Les Liaisons Dangereuses*, Penguin
    Classics. (Don't worry, it's in English.)
Alfred Stuart Nuyers, *Letters for All Occasions*, Harper
    Perennial.
Rainer Maria Rilke, *Letters to a Young Poet*, Vintage Press.
John Stiker and Andrew Shapiro, *Superthreats: How to
    Sound Like a Lawyer and Get Your Rights on Your
    Own*, Rawson Associates.
William Strunk and E. B. White, *The Elements of Style*,
    Macmillan.

CHAPTER 9

Lab
Reports

W hy the heck does your teacher want you to write a lab report detailing your experiment anyway? You may think it is a sneaky way to prove that you have actually done the experiment. If, however, you take a moment to consider the parts of a lab report, you will see a larger truth emerge. You write a lab report so you can indicate your personal thought process as it relates to the experiment or study performed. For instance, you might have dissolved aspirin until it became wintergreen oil, but it makes no difference if you did this or exploded marshmallows in the microwave unless you understand *why* you did it, and what the results mean.

Experimentation is often misunderstood. You may have heard things like, "The experiment was unsuccessful; we have failed in our mission." Don't worry about "failing." An experiment is an attempt to discover how something will react in a given situation. Since you will always discover something, the experiment is always a success, even if what you find out annoys you. You write a lab report to say what you thought you might observe, then what you did observe, and what you think it all means. So whether you notice, like Sir Alexander Fleming, that there's a tiny mold that's destroying all the other stuff in your petri dish, or you notice that when you add substance A to substance B not a darn thing happens, you have something to write down and a great lab report to deliver. As long as you know why you were performing the experiment in the first place, and what the results show you, your experiment is a success.

FORMAT

While individual teachers or professors may have particular specifications, the general format for a lab report is as follows:

PURPOSE OF EXPERIMENT
This is the first paragraph of your report, and contains exactly what it says. Why are you doing your experiment? What do you hope to find or discover? The answer to these questions is your purpose, which gives the experiment and your observations a context.

MATERIALS
List the materials and their amounts in case, after you're gone, someone wants to replicate your findings.

STEP-BY-STEP PROCESS OF EXPERIMENT
Write exactly what happened in chronological order: what actions you performed and what you observed to follow from these actions. When you have the opportunity, illustrate your process with cunning drawings. Some teachers will require that this section be laid out numerically as in step one, step two, and so on. Others will prefer that you present this section in paragraph form.

OUTCOME, DISCUSSION OF OUTCOME, CONCLUSIONS
Here is where the purpose of your experiment and the observations come together. If the results were as you expected, say what that means and why the results are as they are. If the results were other than what you had expected, explain why, if you can. If you don't know why you achieved the results you did, offer some hypotheses. Conclude with a statement indicating how this experiment and the results you observed furthered your understanding of what you studied.

Make sure you check this outline with the requirements of your class. Most lab reports will include at least these basic requirements.

HOW TO WRITE THE DARN THING, WITH NELL

STEP 1: DECIDE ON THE EXPERIMENT AND READ ANY BACKGROUND MATERIAL

Usually, you write a lab report based on experiments you perform in school. If you have to select your own experiment, make it something you want to explore. Can too many fish sticks really make you sick? Which is better, Coke or Pepsi? What really happens when you put marshmallows in the microwave?

Nell, a brilliant and enterprising young scientist, will conduct her experiment at home because she is extremely motivated and was told she can earn extra credit by doing so. She has always had the feeling that her dogs understand what she says to them; now is her opportunity to test this out. She will attempt to discover whether dogs understand what people are saying. She has an eerie feeling they do, and she has planned an experiment to help her prove it. She has three dogs: Geoff, Almon and Mike. She is going to use Geoff as

> a control group and the others as subjects. She will read Almon the same calming story every day, she will read Mike sad dog stories every day for five days, and she will simply observe Geoff at the same time each day, without his having been read a story. Daily, she will record all the dogs' responses.

If your experiment is assigned in class, you will probably be assigned a chapter to read. READ IT! If you don't know why you are conducting the experiment, you will have a tough time grasping the concepts, staying interested, and writing a decent lab report.

STEP 2: ASSEMBLE AND LIST YOUR MATERIALS

When you are performing experiments, orderliness is extremely important. If you are not exact, your results will be suspect, so try to be careful. Write down everything you have set up before you start your process.

> Nell takes out her notebook and writes down the following:
>
> Almon (Chocolate Lab)
> Mike (Lovable mutt)
> Geoff (Spaniel)
> Audio tapes of happy dog stories
> Audio tapes of unhappy dog stories
> Tape Player
> Notebook for observations
> Special closed off room for observations

STEP 3: PERFORM YOUR EXPERIMENT, TAKING NOTES

To write a complete lab report you must make accurate observations WHILE you perform your experiment, even if that means just writing down, "The mixture is turning blue and fizzy, it is overflowing out of the beaker, the desk has caught fire, must go." Be as descriptive and accurate as possible; these notes will form the bulk of your report.

> Nell marks Day One in her notebook, and takes Almon into the observation room where she plays the tape of *See Spot Run.* She marks down everything Almon does. She then removes Almon and repeats the process for Mike, playing him the same tape, then takes Geoff into the room and observes him while not playing a tape. Day two she plays the tape of *See Spot Run* for Almon, one of the unhappy dog stories for Mike, and again no tape for Geoff. For the next five days she plays the *See Spot Run* tape for Almon, a different unhappy dog story tape for Mike, and no tape at all for Geoff, noting that Mike seems to get happier and happier, and Almon seems to become more agitated. She marks down these observations and ponders them.

STEP 4: WRITING

Once you have performed the experiment and taken notes, writing your lab report will be easy. Follow the format referred to on pages 142–143. First, write the introduction and purpose of the experiment, then the materials, then the observations, then the conclusions and any appropriate comments.

DOGS AND LITERATURE

by Nell

The purpose of my experiment was to test whether my dogs can, as I believe they can, understand what I say to them. I tested this theory by recording three dogs' responses to calming texts read aloud, both calming and upsetting texts read aloud, and no texts read. Three dogs, Geoff, Almon, and Mike were my subjects. Geoff was not read to at all, Almon was read a soothing dog text—*See Spot Run*—and Mike was read a variety of unhappy dog texts. All the dogs reactions were monitored to determine whether they corresponded to the text read. The hypothesis was, if the dogs understood what they heard, they should have been fine and relaxed through the calm text, upset by the upsetting text, and unaffected by the absence of any reading or speech.

MATERIALS

Mike—Lovable mutt, aged 2 years, weight 15 pounds.

Almon—Chocolate Lab, aged 2 years, six months, weight 60 pounds.

Geoff—Spaniel, aged 3 years, weight 21 pounds.

Audio Recordings of:

See Spot Run—Happy Dog Story

Cujo—Unhappy Dog Story

Champ, Gallant Collie—Unhappy Dog Story

The Spotted Dotted Puppy—Unhappy Dog Story

101 Dalmatians—Unhappy Dog Story, Ultimate Triumph Excluded

Figure 1

| Almon | Mike | Geoff |

PROCEDURE

Day One

Almon: Played tape of *See Spot Run*, a happy dog story, for fifteen minutes. Almon walked around room for 4 minutes, scratched himself for 7.5 minutes, yawned 4 times, wagged his tail for 3.5 minutes.

Mike: Played tape of *See Spot Run* for fifteen minutes. Received same general responses, 8 minutes of scratching, 5 minutes of walking around room sniffing things, 3 minutes of tail-wagging and 5 yawns.

Geoff: Played no tape and did not speak to him. He napped for 15 minutes.

Day Two

Almon: Played tape of *See Spot Run* for Almon for 15 minutes. Almon walked and sniffed for 5 minutes this time, scratched himself for 6 minutes, yawned twice, and stood and wagged his tail for 4 minutes.

Mike: Played audio tape of *Spotted Dotted Puppy,* a story of conformity and abandonment in the animal world. Mike trotted around the room for 8 minutes, wagging his tail, then scratched himself for the remainder of the time (7 minutes). Yawned 3 times.

Geoff: Played no tape and did not speak to him. He napped for 15 minutes.

Day Three

Almon: Played tape of *See Spot Run* for Almon for 15 minutes. Almon walked around the room for 2 minutes, then stopped and started growling at the tape recorder during the section in which Jane sees Spot run. The growling continued for 6 minutes, after which Almon started yelping and whining, for 5 minutes. The final 2 minutes Almon alternately scratched his ear vigorously and whined.

Mike: Played audio tape of *Champ, Gallant Collie.* Watched closely, particularly section during which Champ is attacked by a mountain lion and almost loses entire herd of sheep. Mike walked and sniffed for 7 minutes, yawned 3 times, wagged his tail for 6 minutes, and scratched himself for 3 minutes.

Geoff: Played no tape and did not speak to him. He napped, woke up after 8.5 minutes, yawned, and returned to napping.

Day Four

Almon: [Note: Almon seemed reluctant to enter the room today.] Played tape of *See Spot Run* for Almon for 15 minutes. There was no tail-wagging at all for the second day in a row, and a repetition of yesterday's growling episode lasted for 11 minutes. The final 4 minutes consisted of Almon lying on the floor and shuffling along on his front paws, whining.

Mike: Played Mike a tape of *Cujo* for 15 minutes. Paid particular attention as a section was played in which a slobbering, rabid Cujo is beaten to death with an axe handle. Mike trotted around the room for 8 minutes, wagging his tail, then scratched himself for the remainder of the time (7 minutes). Yawned 3 times.

Geoff: Played no tape and did not speak to him. He napped for 15 minutes.

Day Five

Almon: Almon had to be physically dragged into the listening room today. Played tape of *See Spot Run* for Almon for 15 minutes. Almon spent the entire 15 minutes howling over the sound of the tape in a mournful and aggrieved manner.

Mike: Played Mike tape of *One Hundred and One Dalmatians*, the excerpt in which Cruella De Ville outlines her plans to make a coat from puppy skins. Mike sniffed and walked for 5.5 minutes, sat and wagged his tail for 5.5 minutes, and rested for 4 minutes, yawned 3 times.

Geoff: Played no tape and did not speak to him. He napped for 15 minutes.

Figure 2

    Almon   Mike   Geoff

CONCLUSION

The results were not exactly what I had anticipated. I hypothesized that hearing the upsetting stories would affect Mike in such a way that he expressed anxiety, yet he remained essentially the same day after day. Almon, on the other, hand, who I expected to remain the same, as he was being read the same thing day after day, expressed extreme anxiety, as can be clearly seen in figure 2. Geoff remained the same day after day, which allows me to understand that there was no outside influence such as a coming storm or a change in diet, to account for the various responses of Almon and Mike. I conclude from this that dogs probably don't understand the words they are being read, but

I believe this experiment provides evidence to justify further experimentation as to whether dogs recognize repetitive sounds, as was so clearly demonstrated by Almon's response to the *Spot* tape day after day. Thus, though I cannot say I have proven that dogs understand English, I can say that I have opened the door to future scientific inquiry.

STEP 5: PROOFREAD

Check back to see that all illustrations and charts are correctly numbered and easily understood. Check for spelling, grammar, and punctuation. Also make sure that your purpose of the experiment was clear, and that your conclusion is well-founded.

COMMON LAB REPORT PITFALLS

CONFUSING

Many students and novice science writers fall into the trap of thinking that science writing must be both boring and loaded with technical terms in order to qualify as science writing. Not so! Like all other writing, science writing is meant to be read. And you can bet your instructor will be happier the better-written your report is.

DULL

Finding out what happens when you pour sulfuric acid over a candy bar, or whatever your particular experiment is, can be really interesting. That's why scientists of old started all of this: they wanted to know what would happen. Sure, everyone else in the class is doing the same experiment, but your perspective and interest in the result are your own. The more you can get interested, the more interesting your report will be.

NO VISUALS

The great thing about lab reports is that, unlike other pieces of writing for school, you can put in pictures. Don't let this fabulous opportunity escape you! You remember those stencils of beakers and flasks on your protractor? This is why they are there, to allow you to express your fabulous creativity in scientific form. Throw in a sketch of yourself performing the experiment, or a sketch of the setup of the titration, or whatever.

LACK OF PURPOSE

Since the point of a lab report is to present your experiment and why you did it, if you don't exactly know why you did it, your lab report will make NO SENSE AT ALL! There are some who write a lab report without this crucial knowledge, so their lab reports become an odd listing of things they did in science class that day, without any understanding of why they did them. Don't let this happen to you. The best way to avoid lack of purpose is to look at the material your teacher or professor gave you with your lab assignment. Why do they want you to do the assignment? If you don't really know, ask questions. Then set up an outline, including a description of the experiment and why you performed it. Did everything happen the way you had expected or predicted it would? If not, why do you think that might be? Know what you mean before you start writing, and your lab report will be much easier to write.

SPECIFICS

FORMAT

Some lab reports accept a numbered list of steps rather than a sentence-by-sentence paragraph for the procedures section.

ROUGH DRAFTS

Generally, lab reports don't go through the rigorous draft process that essays and research papers are subjected to. Before you hand your lab report in, you should still proofread it for any possible errors, but the full-fledged stylistic editing process is generally used more on scientific research papers, which are formatted like regular research papers and are edited as such.

TITLE

Always include a title page. It gives you the opportunity to be clever, and you can use more fabulous visual aids.

REFERENCES

Unless your instructor requests one, there is generally no need to supply a bibliography or any other list of reference sources. If you do use a quote from someone's work, supply the name of the author and the title in parentheses within the report.

AMOUNTS

When listing materials, be sure to include amounts so the exact proportions can be deduced.

AND THUS...

Lab reports benefit from lucid prose. Your reports will shine when you understand your experiment before you begin writing and express what you mean as clearly as you can.

BOOK LIST

The following books discuss science in a clear exciting way understandable to the non-scientist. Read, enjoy, and emulate.

Isaac Asimov, *Isaac Asimov's Guide to Earth and Space*, Fawcett.
Rachel Carson, *Silent Spring*, Houghton Mifflin.
James Gleick, *Chaos*, The Penguin Group.
Stephen Jay Gould, *Bully for Brontosaurus*, Norton.
David MacCauley, *The Way Things Work*, Houghton Mifflin.
John McPhee, *In Suspect Terrain*, The Noonday Press.
Lewis Thomas, *The Lives of a Cell*, Bantam Books.
Lewis Thomas, *The Medusa and the Snail*, G.K. Hall and Company.

CHAPTER 10

Project
Proposals

Maybe you need to present some great idea to your employer, so you call her on the phone and she says, "Give it to me in writing and I'll take a look at it, I have no time to listen now." Or maybe you are applying for a grant and need to outline your project to demonstrate how worthwhile it is, and how much you and your project, in particular, deserve the money. A project proposal is a written description of your project along with a rationale for why it should be undertaken or funded.

Whatever the occasion for your proposal, don't panic. Project proposals are simple to put together. All you need is an idea, some energy, some organization, and, if possible, some visuals.

FORMAT

INTRODUCTION
This should state how your idea came to be; if your project is to satisfy some hole in the array of products in the world, here you can write, "It was always clear to me that there were not enough different types of cookie jars in the world." Then, describe your project and how it will address that need.

BODY OF PROPOSAL
This section will always be divided into three parts.

The Idea: Here you will outline the basics of your idea.
Your Plan: What you will do once the money or project is awarded to you.
You: Your particular qualifications for the task or project at hand.

PARTICULARS
These are not absolutely necessary, but it may be helpful to itemize the costs and needs of your project here.

CONCLUSION
Here you provide a stirring argument for why your idea is so great, and a graceful signing off.

HOW TO WRITE A PROPOSAL, WITH MIMI AND LISA

STEP 1: THE OUTLINE

You first need to organize your thoughts, and as we have seen before, the best way to do that is to write an outline. An outline for a project proposal gives you a chance to write down your idea and organize how you will sell it.

Lisa and Mimi have an idea; they want someone to give them money so they can travel around the world for a few years by boat, having a wonderful time. They call this project the Sailing Sirens. They figure they need five million dollars. A long shot perhaps, but they are putting together a proposal and sending it around. Not only do they want to write a proposal for this project, but they also want to write the proposal together, which makes it a collaborative project. Yet they have no fear; they know that if you start with a clear plan, collaborative writing can be less work and more fun than writing alone.

To begin, both write outlines, which they can then compare and meld into one.

Lisa's Outline

I. Introduction: Why? There aren't enough women having fun out there, there is a great need for a few raise-hell women
   A. evidence for this, success of *Thelma and Louise*, the movie of women raising hell
   B. people's undying interest in the antics of supermodels
   C. success of "Absolutely Fabulous," British television series in which a couple of hellions tear up the town
   D. Sailing Sirens: we want to have fun.
II. Idea: Me and Mimi on a boat with plenty of money and a radio; the possibilities are endless

    A. a couple of scenarios?
      Mimi and I swim in the Aegean
      Mimi and I disrupt a boring meeting and create
      an international incident
      Mimi and I skydive in Venezuela
    B. When we get the money, we buy the boat and
      set sail
    C. Why us? Mimi has sailed before, we are ready
      for this kind of fun.
III. Costs
    How much the boat, the food, etc. will cost
IV. Conclusion
    How great it will be to have this need filled and
    how worthy a cause it is

Mimi's Outline

I. Introduction
    <u>Why</u>? There is no record of women taking a trip like
    this.
    <u>Idea</u>: Sailing Sirens—me and Lisa take a boat and
    sail and sail and sail, island to island, then write
    a book
II. Idea
    A. The Plan: We outline the plan of going from island
      to island, starting on Martha's Vineyard, then
      south, then east. Give an example of the kind
      of entry we would write.
    B. With the money we first do research about other
      island-to-island boat jaunts, throughout history,
      then buy a boat, then itinerary
    C. Why us? We are interested in women and history
      and the history of travel, we can do the island-
      to-island thing with an historical perspective,
      we can write a book about it
III. Conclusion: how worthy it would be to have this kind
    of travel history done by women, right now.

They get together and compare notes and flip their respective wigs. Their outlines are so different! Their ideas for the trip are so divergent! Or are they? They spend some time discussing the particulars of each of their proposals. Do they really want to make a book of this? Is it for fun or for historical importance, and is there a difference between these two things?

This discussion and comparison of goals is of the utmost importance for anyone planning a collaborative writing project. It allows you to compare ideas and really come up with a common focus, *before* the bulk of the writing is done.

Lisa and Mimi first try to decide whether they really do want to write a book about their adventures. Mimi confesses that she included that section in her outline because she wanted to sound worthier of funding. Lisa says that, actually, they don't need to sound worthy of funding, they *are* worthy of funding. Why pretend to be scholars when they are not? They have other attributes, and their project is not about books.

Next to be decided is the perspective of the trip. Is it for fun or for history? Again, they talk about what they really want to do. They decide that what they really want is not to talk about travel but to have some fun. They consider for some time and decide to focus on the hell-raising women aspect of the trip; they want to do this to have a good time, why shouldn't that be their strength? And, after all, they want to be honest about the money they seek. Mimi volunteers to write the final outline for the proposal, which Lisa will then check over.

Final Outline

I. Introduction
   <u>Why</u>: There is a great need for images of women being daring and reckless. The public is hungry for it, witness
   A. success of *Thelma and Louise*, the movie of women raising hell
   B. people's undying interest in the antics of supermodels
   C. success of "Absolutely Fabulous," British television series in which a couple of hellions tear up the town
   <u>Therefore</u>: We will go on a no-holds-barred ocean-going tour.

II. Plan
   <u>Idea</u>: We will buy a sailboat and adventure across the open seas, inspiring all who hear tell of us.
   <u>Scenarios</u>
   A. skydiving in Venezuela
   B. swimming in the Aegean
   C. barging into a meeting and creating an international incident
   <u>How</u>: You will give us money, we will buy a boat and go where the winds take us.
   <u>Why us</u>: We have the time, the inclination, the wild woman credentials.

III. Conclusion
   It's really a great idea.

STEP 2: CHECK YOUR OUTLINE

Read your outline and try to determine if it gives you a clear writing plan. Do you know the main gist of what you want to get across? Do you understand what you will write? If so, continue. If not, rework your outline until it fulfills these guidelines.

STEP 3: GATHER YOUR DATA AND WRITE A ROUGH DRAFT

A good project proposal is one that is based on diligent research, and reflects that diligent research. If you are competing with others for a project, point out your past success rate, or their statistical weaknesses. If you are demonstrating a need for strawberry pizza that you are going to fill, note that there were over one million calls for strawberry pizza recorded by Pizza Hut.

Once you have gathered as many facts and figures as you can—by using the library, the Chamber of Commerce, the Internet, and any other information source that occurs to you—you can begin writing. Writing a project proposal is much like writing a research paper. You follow your outline, paragraph by paragraph, and put together a rough draft to work from. When you are working collaboratively, you might assign one person research and the other writing. Another possibility is to assign separate sections of the outline to each person. For instance, the introduction and the idea sections might go to one person, and the conclusion and the other paragraphs to the other. This second option can be difficult when you are putting the whole proposal together, because often people have different writing styles, and putting the pieces together will entail trying to make the whole proposal stylistically uniform. Whichever option you select, make these decisions based on strengths and weaknesses. Whoever is the better writer should write more, and whoever is the better "talker" should speak during meetings, or however the strengths and weaknesses fall. Try to determine this division of labor ahead of time, as negotiations in the middle of writing can make an already difficult task more trying.

> Mimi and Lisa decide that Lisa will be responsible for the research, and Mimi will write the proposal, which will then be edited and revised by Lisa. Lisa goes to the library and finds books about adventuring women, women sailors, and sea-going. She calls the Motion Picture Association of America and finds out how many people went to see *Thelma and Louise*. Meanwhile, Mimi sits on the veranda, sips lemonade, and thinks of convincing images to put in her writing. When Lisa has accumulated enough facts, she gives her copious and well-organized notes to Mimi, who then goes inside to her word processor while Lisa sits on the veranda with a toast of chocolate milk.

STEP 4: EDIT

Edit your proposal, aiming to make it professional, convincing, and clear. You know what to do, and if you need reminding, check back to the editing questions in chapter four.

One more time! Edit Mimi's rough draft, looking for clarity, organization, and brevity. When you're done, see if Lisa's edits agree with yours.

Rough Draft

Everyone craves adventure. Executives tucked away in offices, professors stranded in ivy covered buildings, doctors overworked in emergency rooms, parents exhausted from car-pooling; all of them dream of mountain climbing or deep-sea diving or traveling through Amazon jungles. Everyone craves adventure, but most people find it vicariously. People want images of adventurous people to inspire them, and consider how many of those executives, professors, doctors and parents are women. There is a lack of daring images of women, and people are willing to pay for them when they can find them. Consider the success of Thelma & Louise, a film of women finding adventure on the open road. Women did not commence to go out on shooting sprees, but they flocked in droves to see the movie; it was one of the seven most popular films of 1991. Yet it was the only reckless kick-butt female adventure film made over the next two years. Consider the public's interest in the antics of supermodels: "What are they doing now? What will they do next? Where are they now?" The supermodels tramp over Europe masking money, breaking hearts and painting the towns red, and people hang on their every bad girl move. In Absolutely Fabulous, the cult hit of British television, a couple of women tear up London, leaving chaos and nail polish in their wake. There are bootleg tapes of this series being sold all over the United States. How to address this need? We propose to buy a boat and take a free-wheeling ocean going tour.

We propose to buy a sturdy ocean going sail boat and adventure across the open seas. We will go from island to continent to island, taking risks and kicking butt. We will swim in the jewel-like waters if the Mediterranean and scale the cliffs of Dover. What are the benefits? We will be sky-diving in Venezuela and then we will sail off to Saint Thomas. A young boy will say, "Wow. The thought of that makes me so happy I will not throw this bowl of mashed peas on the floor but will instead wait for my mother to take it from my high chair." We will be swimming in the Aegean Sea and a politician in her office will pick up her pen and say, "Gosh, the idea of them swimming makes me so thrilled I will sign this treaty ending all war everywhere." We will storm into a meeting in Portugal and everyone will talk about it for days, instead of harping on the drab details of some actor's divorce, thus sparing both the public and the actor. Aside from these benefits to the public, we will be having a wonderful time, and in doing so, will provide the world of women with role models, with an idea of how to live life on the edge and to the fullest.

We will accomplish this plan with a grant of $5,000,000.

First we will buy the boat, and some necessary luggage, rations, and navigating charts. The money that remains after this will be used as spending money so we can instruct the world on how to buy without remorse, and live life as it should be lived. We will have no set itinerary, as that would work against our philosophy and our mission. We will probably set sail from Martha's Vineyard in Massachusetts, and there's no telling where we will go next. We will simply sail and land and land and sail, striking fear in the hearts of the sedate and thrilling women everywhere. It is hoped that we will circumnavigate the globe within three years.

We are well qualified for such an rigorous task. Mimi is an experienced para-sailor and deep-sea diver, who has inspired masses to abandon work in the middle of the day and go swimming. Of the six employers she has had in the last three years, all six have said, after she left employment to seek adventure somewhere else, "She's a real pistol. I'm inspired." She received her first class captain's license in 1989 and has undertaken over thirty month-long journeys with other people's boats. Lisa can knock a thimble off a rattlesnake's head at fifty yards with a bow and arrow. She has climbed to the top of Mount Kilimanjaro twice, and was awarded with citations for bravery by the Parks Association. Her niece says, "Lisa is a wild hell-cat. I hope I can be like her when I grow up." Both Lisa and Mimi are members of I'm Going To Have A Good Time If It Kills Me, an association whose members have enjoyed themselves in unlikely places ranging from high school dances to Sociology doctoral programs.

There is both the need and the opportunity to have some women running wild in these trying times. Society needs this, the balance of the world needs it, and we need it. We can have a good enough time for every person on earth; you can help us to do so. Two women in a sailboat whooping it up can only help the state of the world, and we ask you to fund this project. It's a worthy cause.

With Lisa's Edits

Everyone craves adventure. Executives tucked away in offices, professors stranded in ivy‿covered buildings, doctors overworked in emergency rooms, parents exhausted from car-pooling; all (of)

unnecessary pronoun (them) dream of mountain climbing or deep-sea diving or traveling

through Amazon jungles. Everyone craves adventure, but most people find it vicariously. People want images of adventurous people to inspire them, and consider how many of those executives, professors, doctors and parents are women. There is a lack of daring images of women, and people are willing to pay for them when they can find them. Consider the success of [Thelma & Louise] a film of women finding adventure on the open road. Women did not commence to go out on shooting sprees, but they flocked in droves to see the movie; it was one of the seven most popular films of 1991. Yet it was the only reckless kick-butt female adventure film made over the next two years. Consider the public's interest in the antics of supermodels: "What are they doing now? What will they do next? Where are they now?" The supermodels tramp over Europe masking money, breaking hearts and painting the towns red, and people hang on their every bad girl move. In Absolutely Fabulous, the cult hit of British

wordy

television, a couple of women tear up London, leaving chaos and nail polish in their wake. There are bootleg tapes of this series being sold all over the United States. How to address this need? We propose to buy a boat and take a free-wheeling ocean-going tour.

link to increased demand for such

italicize film titles

quotes on television shows

more than one "need"?

can we

obvious

We propose to buy a (sturdy) ocean going sail boat and adventure   =/

across the open seas. We will (go) from island to continent to island,   *more*

taking risks and kicking butt. We will swim in the jewel-like waters   *specific*
                                                                        verb

typo   (if) the Mediterranean and scale the cliffs of Dover. What are the

"to others"   benefits? We will be sky-diving in Venezuela and then we will sail

off to Saint Thomas. A young boy will say, "Wow. The thought of   (lc)

that makes me so happy I will not throw this bowl of mashed peas on

the floor but will instead wait for my mother to take it from my high

chair." We will be swimming in the Aegean Sea and a politician in
                                                        those two women
her office will pick up her pen and say, "Gosh, the idea of them

swimming makes me so thrilled I will sign this treaty ending all war

everywhere." We will storm into a meeting in Portugal and everyone
what?
need   will talk about (it) for days, instead of harping on the drab details of
clear
reference   some actor's divorce, thus sparing both the public and the actor.   *unclear*
                                                                        tense,
Aside from these benefits to the public, we (will be having) a   *fix*

wonderful time, and in doing so, will provide the world of women   *no! the*
                                                                    whole world!
with role models, with an idea of how to live life on the edge and to

the fullest.

We will accomplish this plan with a grant of $5,000,000. First we

will buy the boat, and (some necessary) luggage, rations, and   *obvious*

navigating charts. The money that remains after this will be used as

spending money so we can instruct the world on how to buy without

remorse, and live life as it should be lived. We will have no set

itinerary, as that would work against our philosophy and our mission.

We will probably set sail from Martha's Vineyard in Massachusetts,

and there's no telling where we will go next.

make
point
clear,
not just
women,
people

We will simply sail and land and land an sail, striking fear in the
hearts of the sedate and thrilling ~~women~~ *people* everywhere. It is hoped
that we will circumnavigate the globe within three years.

We are well qualified for such an rigorous task. Mimi is an
experienced para-sailor and deep-sea diver, who has inspired
masses to abandon work in the middle of the day and go
swimming. Of the six employers she has had in the last three years,

redundant,
unnecessary

all (six) have said, after she left employment to seek adventure
somewhere else, "She's a real pistol. I'm inspired." She received
her first class captain's license in 1989 and has undertaken over
thirty month-long journeys with other people's boats. Lisa can
knock a thimble off a rattlesnake's head at fifty yards with a bow
and arrow. She has climbed to the top of Mount Kilimanjaro twice,
and was awarded with citations for bravery by the Parks

be specific ————————— *Dana*

Association. Her niece says, "Lisa is a wild hell-cat. I hope I can be
like her when I grow up." Both Lisa and Mimi are members of [I'm   — *itals*
Going To Have A Good Time If It Kills Me,] an association whose
members have enjoyed themselves in unlikely places ranging from
High School dances to Sociology doctoral programs.

repeat for
emphasis

There is both the need and the opportunity to have some women
                                                          it
running wild in these trying times. Society needs ~~this,~~ the balance
of the world needs it, and we need it. We can have a good enough
                                          and
time for every person on earth; you can help us to do so. Two
women in a sailboat whooping it up can only help the state of the
world, and we ask you to fund this project. It's a worthy cause.

STEP 5: PUT IT ALL TOGETHER

Your proposal should be as professional as possible, so make double
checks for typos, grammar, and spelling mistakes. The language should
be clear and convincing, while conveying your enthusiasm for the
project at hand.

The title page of your proposal should indicate to the recipients what they are to expect, and from whom. You should also include information on how the recipients can get in touch with you, though that same information should be included in your cover letter; see chapter eight on professional letters.

Keys to the success of a proposal are much like those of a business letter: brevity and knowledge of your audience. The cover letter of a proposal should be no longer than one page, and should include a brief description of the project and the amount of money requested. Also, like other professional letters, indicate any previous contact with the funding source, and why you chose this particular funding source to approach.

> Lisa and Mimi have discussed the edits made on the previous pages and implemented them. They have rewritten the awkward sentences (you should check for those) and cleaned up all typos and spelling. Their proposal, which follows, is now ready to go. In your own proposal you should rely more on facts and figures than they have here, but for their project these were not as relevant. (If you are interested in funding this project, by the way, simply contact the author of this book through the publisher's address.)

Sailing Sirens

A Proposal for a Round-the-World Voyage

Submitted by Lisa Smith and Mimi Smith

1234 Helena Handbasket Drive

Los Angeles, California 90210

(213) 555-5555

Submit to: We Have Money To Burn Inc.,

The People Who Gave You Biospheres One and Two

000 Nowheresville

Tucson, Arizona 88888

Everyone craves adventure. Executives tucked away in offices, professors stranded in ivy-covered buildings, doctors overworked in emergency rooms, parents exhausted from carpooling: all dream of mountain-climbing or deep-sea diving or traveling through Amazon jungles. Everyone craves adventure, but most people find it vicariously. Consider the demand this creates for images of adventure to inspire them. Then consider how many of those executives, professors, doctors, and parents are women. There is a lack of daring images of women, and people are willing to pay for them when they can find them. Consider the success of *Thelma and Louise*, a film of women finding adventure on the open road. Women did not commence to go out on shooting sprees, but they flocked in droves to see the movie; it was one of the seven most popular films of 1991. Yet it was the only reckless kick-butt female adventure film made over the next two years. Consider the public's interest in the antics of supermodels: "What are they doing now? What will they do next? Where are they now?" The supermodels tramp over Europe making money, breaking hearts, and painting towns red, and people hang on their every bad girl move. In "Absolutely Fabulous," the cult hit of British television, a pair of women tear up London, leaving chaos and nail polish in their wake. There are over 250,000 bootleg tapes of this series being sold all over the United States. How can we address these needs? We propose to buy a boat and take a freewheeling oceangoing tour.

We propose to buy an oceangoing sailboat and adventure across the open seas. We will sail from island to continent to island, taking risks and kicking butt. We will swim in the jewel-like waters of the Mediterranean and scale the cliffs of Dover. What are the benefits to the rest of the world? We will sky-dive in Venezuela, and a young boy will say, "Wow. The thought of that makes me so happy I will not throw this bowl of mashed peas on the floor but will instead wait for my mother to take it from my high chair." We will swim in the Aegean Sea and a politician in her office will pick up her pen and say, "Gosh, the idea of those two women swimming makes me so thrilled I will sign this treaty ending all war everywhere." We will storm into a meeting in Portugal and everyone will talk about the spectacle for days, instead of harping on the drab details of some actor's divorce, thus sparing both the public and the actor. Aside from these benefits to the public, we will have a wonderful time, and in doing so, will provide the world with role models, with an idea of how to live life on the edge and to the fullest.

We will accomplish this plan with a grant of $5,000,000. First we will buy the boat, luggage, rations, and navigating charts. The money that remains after this will be used as spending money so we can instruct the world on how to buy without remorse, and live life as it should be lived. We will have no set itinerary, as that would work against our philosophy and our mission. We will probably set sail from Martha's Vineyard in Massachusetts, and there's no telling where we will go next. We will simply sail and land, and land and sail, striking fear in the hearts of the sedate, and thrilling people everywhere.

We are well qualified for such a rigorous task. Mimi is an experienced para-sailor and deep-sea diver, who has inspired masses to abandon work in the middle of the day and go swimming. Of the six employers she has had in the last three years, all have said, after she left employment to seek adventure somewhere else, "She's a real pistol. I'm inspired." She received her first-class captain's license in 1989 and has undertaken over thirty month-long journeys with other people's boats. Lisa can knock a thimble off a rattlesnake's head at fifty yards with a bow and arrow. She has climbed to the top of Mount Kilimanjaro twice, and was awarded with citations for bravery by the Parks Association. Her niece Dana says, "Lisa is a wild hellcat. I hope I can be like her when I grow up." Both Lisa and Mimi are members of *I'm Going To Have A Good Time If It Kills Me*, an association whose members have enjoyed themselves in unlikely places ranging from high school dances to Sociology doctoral programs.

There is both the need and the opportunity to have some women running wild in these trying times. Society needs it, the balance of the world needs it, and we need it. We can have a good enough time for every person on earth, and you can help us do so. Two women in a sailboat whooping it up can only help the state of the world, and we ask you to fund this project. It's a worthy cause.

STEP 6: HAND IT IN

The nice thing about project proposals is that you can put them in those fancy celluloid binders and cardboard covers. Don't go overboard with your presentation, just make sure what you submit is neat and professional.

COMMON PROJECT PROPOSAL PITFALLS

LACK OF SUBSTANTIATION

When you write a project proposal you must sell your idea, and as with all selling, the buyer is constantly wary of being taken. Give buyers, or readers, sufficient evidence; your enthusiasm must be backed up with fact.

NO VISUALS

If you can convince someone more easily with a chart depicting evidence visually, by all means do so. Charts, graphs, and photographs contribute to a proposal's professional look, and break up the text to make it more interesting.

LACK OF PROFESSIONALISM

There are no allowances made for eccentricity or creative license in a project proposal. If you do not appear entirely capable and well-organized, readers will not trust you. Remember, you are asking readers to give you either money or control of some project, all of which makes recipients understandably nervous. It is your job to convince them of your reliability.

SENDING IT TO THE WRONG PEOPLE

Know your audience. If you are trying to sell a book about your experiences in the wilderness, don't send your proposal to a crossword puzzle publisher. This affects the way you write the proposal as well. Are you trying to convince an arts commissioner? Then your proposal should focus on that aspect of your work.

BORING

Always a danger, in any kind of writing. If you truly believe your idea is exciting, make sure your enthusiasm is conveyed, not in a "rah rah" high school way, but by communicating how strongly you believe in yourself and your work. Most businesses receive hundreds of proposals, yours should stand out.

SPECIFICS

ALWAYS PROVIDE A TITLE PAGE

This should include to whom the proposal is being submitted, and your name, address, and where you can be reached. If it is a group project, it should list the name of the group or association writing the project, and the name of one person whom they can contact for questions and correspondence.

FOOTNOTE ALL REFERENCES

The more documented backup you have, the better your proposal looks.

NUMBER CHARTS, GRAPHS, AND ILLUSTRATIONS

Number them so you can refer to them clearly in the text.

AND THUS...

The best project proposals, like the best of any other type of writing, are clear, cogent, and well-researched. As long as you take the time to organize and carefully edit your presentation, you should be able to put together a proposal that presents your ideas clearly and convinces a reader that you are the proper one for any job, project, or funding at hand.

BOOK LIST

The following books are written especially for the business writer, and are invaluable for their information on structure, style, and presentation.

William Paxson, *The Business Writing Handbook*, Bantam Books, 1981.
William Paxson, *Principles of Style for the Business Writer*, Dodd, Mead & Company, 1985.

Some
Final
Words

Y ou now have the necessary tools to write anything for any instructor or professional situation. The more you write, the more your writing will improve. If you must write some piece that is not covered in this book, bear in mind the overall format for any presentation or essay:

Introduction
Examples or Reasons
Conclusion

This formula will work every time.

The best way to improve your writing, other than writing constantly, is to read as much as possible. The more you become familiar with graceful sentences and cogent arguments, the easier it will be to create them in your own work. Look to the recommended reading lists at the end of each chapter, and go exploring on your own. Read magazines and books and comic books; anything that holds your interest can help you hold the interest of others, and most writers' work refers to writers they admire, widening your reading horizons.

Above all, never forget that writing takes work. Edit your writing and put it through as many drafts as needed. Like anything else, diligence and mastery of the rudiments will soon reflect in your work, making it better than you might have thought possible. So good luck, and keep writing.

NOTES

NOTES

NOTES

NOTES

NOTES

NOTES

NOTES

About the Author

Marcia Lerner graduated from Brown University in 1986. She has been teaching and writing for The Princeton Review since 1988. She lives in Brooklyn, NY.

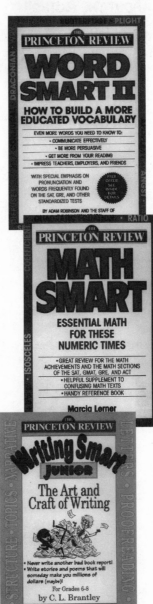